WILTSH
RAILWAYS

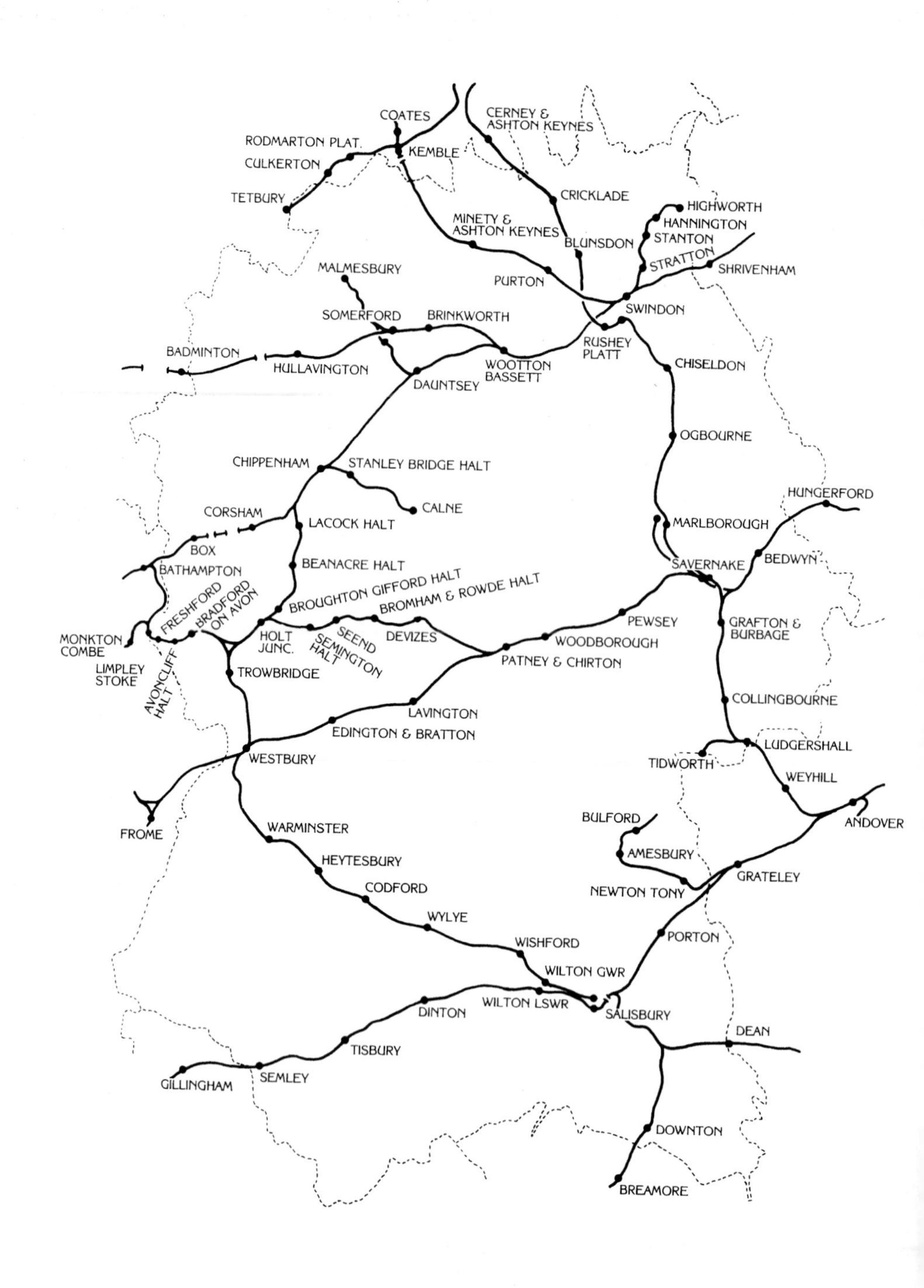
COATES
RODMARTON PLAT.
KEMBLE
CULKERTON
TETBURY
CERNEY & ASHTON KEYNES
CRICKLADE
HIGHWORTH
HANNINGTON
STANTON
MINETY & ASHTON KEYNES
BLUNSDON
STRATTON
SHRIVENHAM
MALMESBURY
PURTON
SWINDON
SOMERFORD
BRINKWORTH
RUSHEY PLATT
BADMINTON
HULLAVINGTON
WOOTTON BASSETT
CHISELDON
DAUNTSEY
OGBOURNE
CHIPPENHAM
STANLEY BRIDGE HALT
HUNGERFORD
CORSHAM
CALNE
LACOCK HALT
MARLBOROUGH
BOX
BEANACRE HALT
SAVERNAKE
BEDWYN
BATHAMPTON
BROUGHTON GIFFORD HALT
BROMHAM & ROWDE HALT
FRESHFORD
BRADFORD ON AVON
PEWSEY
GRAFTON & BURBAGE
MONKTON COMBE
HOLT JUNC.
SEEND
DEVIZES
WOODBOROUGH
SEMINGTON HALT
LIMPLEY STOKE
TROWBRIDGE
PATNEY & CHIRTON
AVONCLIFF HALT
LAVINGTON
COLLINGBOURNE
EDINGTON & BRATTON
LUDGERSHALL
WESTBURY
TIDWORTH
WEYHILL
FROME
BULFORD
ANDOVER
WARMINSTER
AMESBURY
HEYTESBURY
GRATELEY
NEWTON TONY
CODFORD
WYLYE
PORTON
WISHFORD
WILTON GWR
WILTON LSWR
DINTON
SALISBURY
DEAN
TISBURY
GILLINGHAM
SEMLEY
DOWNTON
BREAMORE

WILTSHIRE RAILWAYS

First published 1988
This edition published 2009

The History Press
The Mill, Brimscombe Port
Stroud, Gloucestershire, GL5 2QG
www.thehistorypress.co.uk

British Library Cataloguing in Publication Data.
A catalogue record for this book is available from the British Library.

ISBN 978 0 7524 5465 8

Typesetting and origination by The History Press
Printed in Great Britain

INTRODUCTION

Few events have had such an impact on life in the rural community as the coming of the railways; an impact which even in today's motor-car-dominated age is still present. In the Wiltshire countryside the change from agriculture to an increasingly urban landscape during Victorian times must have been one gazed on with awe by our forbears, even if today the county is still said to possess more sheep than human inhabitants.

Despite its obvious connections with the GWR main line between London and Bristol, the first railway in the county to be fully completed as originally envisaged was in fact the line from Swindon towards Cirencester which carried its first passengers on 31 May 1840. Less than a month later the GWR main line was finished between London and Bristol, to be followed by a succession of branches and connecting routes as well as, later, the important Berks and Hants Extension company's route (the name belies the fact that the line never ventured near to Hampshire) and the Wilts, Somerset & Weymouth scheme.

All these lines were later absorbed under the umbrella heading of the GWR which, as is well known, was to develop what was an insignificant village into the main workshops for the line at Swindon.

But the GWR was not to have the county solely to itself for in 1860 the London & South Western company had pushed its own route west from Salisbury towards Yeovil and Exeter. A few years later in 1883 the independent Midland & South Western Junction system was opened from Cheltenham through Swindon to Marlborough and eventually Andover, a proverbial thorn in the side of the GWR which had up to that time regarded Swindon as almost its own private domain. To say then, that the MSWJ was disliked by the Great Western is an understatement.

The last of the lines to be opened in the county was arguably one of the most important and took the GWR main line west from Wootton Bassett through the southernmost fringe of the Cotswold hills towards Bristol and Wales; a major shortening of the route from London to the Principality.

But despite its undoubted dominance of the county it is not with the GWR that this pictorial approach begins and instead the first few pages are devoted to the South Western, starting from Salisbury. The book then covers some of the other LSWR Wiltshire routes followed by the main GWR route and finally the numerous branches.

Unfortunately in a volume this size it is just not possible to depict every station within the area and the choice has therefore been made to restrict coverage to those locations which happen to be of particular personal interest. I have also taken the opportunity to include a number of documents associated with the contemporary railway scene, with the whole presenting what I hope will be seen as a reflection of the railway heritage of the area.

For the purist there is included at the rear a chronology of the opening dates for the various lines covered although I have deliberately avoided closure dates as these are well chronicled elsewhere.

In the compilation of this album I must record my thanks to Roger Simmonds, Mike Jolly, Peter Squibb and Dennis Tillman. Also to Peter and Judith at the publishers.

Kevin Robertson.
Eastleigh 1988.

DESPITE BEING PRIMARILY A RAILWAY BOOK I make no excuses for the inclusion of this as the first view. The photograph shows what is referred to as the Old Mill House at Salisbury, with the famous cathedral spire in the distance. The view was taken as a GWR publicity photograph no doubt to extol the benefits of a visit to Salisbury – travelling by GWR of course. This was despite the fact that the city was more conveniently reached from London by the rival Southern route and that this had been recognised with a concentration of resources at the former LSWR station some years earlier. (GWR)

A PAIR OF DRUMMOND-DESIGN ENGINES at Salisbury LSWR on a down West of England express. The GWR station was alongside and out of shot to the left whilst the LSWR engine shed was some little way behind the photographer. Although the original print is undated it was probably taken c. 1912 and reflects well the contemporary railway scene when both engines and stations were clean all round, a reflection indeed (no pun intended) on the owning company. (Lens of Sutton.)

THE EXTERIOR OF SALISBURY LSWR STATION, 'down' side, and little altered to the present day. Under a glass it is possible to read the words 'Booking Office' and 'Telegraph Office', the latter a throw-back to the time when the railways would accept telegrams for onward transmission. (Lens of Sutton.)

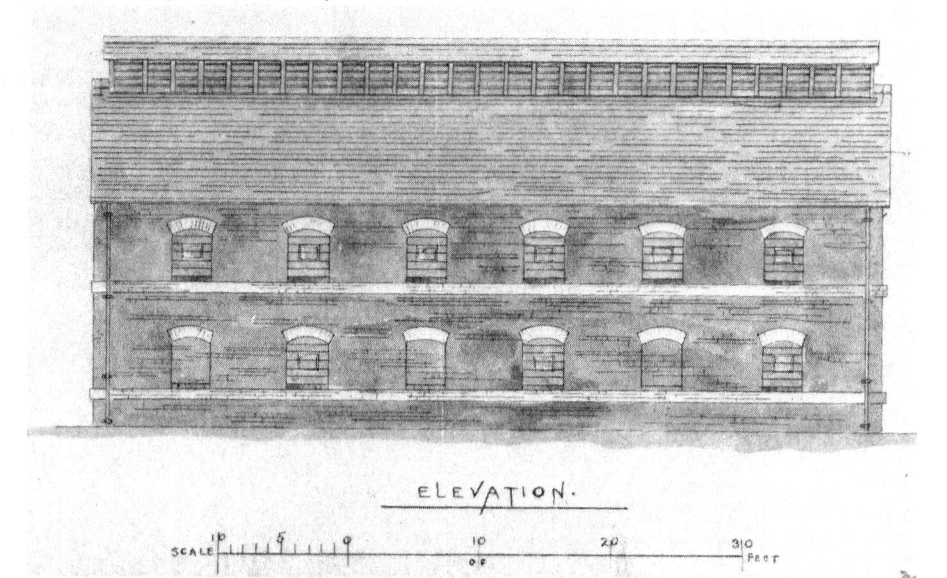

THE NEW ROASTING HOUSE for Messrs Williams at Salisbury station in 1872. As built the structure utilised mellow brickwork under a roof not dissimilar to that of a contemporary engine shed and was almost 60ft. long.

IN THE EARLY YEARS OF THE PRESENT CENTURY the LSWR installed a pneumatic form of signalling at a number of locations including Salisbury. The results were impressive, with the system remaining in use until comparatively recent times. In this view of Salisbury West 'box notice the air reservoir to the left of the building as well as the cylinder at the base of the ground signal. (Author's Collection.)

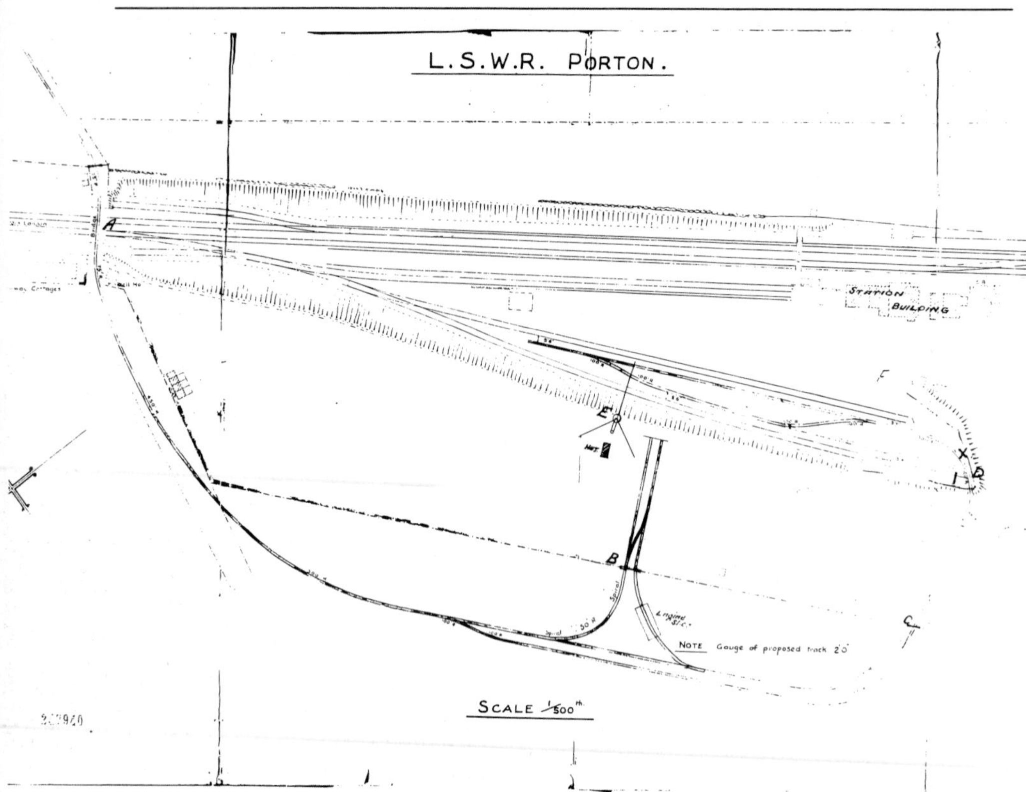

THE TRACK LAYOUT AT PORTON c. 1918, at a time when a proposal was mooted for a narrow gauge military line with connections at the station. This was never built and as a result information on the original need for such a facility is difficult to ascertain.

EAST OF SALISBURY, but still at the moment in Wiltshire, lay part of the route from Alderbury Junction down to West Moors. In this delightful period view of Downton station a southbound train is just entering the loop on a service from Salisbury with an Adams engine at its head. The passing loop at this station was removed in 1922 and relegated to siding status, the single-line section then extending from Breamore, and later Fordingbridge, as far as Alderbury Junction. (Lens of Sutton.)

ANOTHER SUPERB VIEW OF DOWNTON pre–1914, with trains crossing in either direction. Notice in the view the ballast covering the top of the sleepers which was a regular feature of railways in the early years. (Lens of Sutton.)

SOUTH-EAST FROM SALISBURY was the line to Eastleigh via Romsey which, in 1847, was the first railway to reach the city. At the intermediate station of Dean, Adams 4–4–0 No. 557 heads an Eastleigh-bound freight past the signal box and level crossing, probably in the late 1930s. (Lens of Sutton.)

THE NUMBER OF MILITARY GARRISONS ON SALISBURY PLAIN meant it was obvious that eventually rail connections would have to be provided. One of these is shown here at Newton Tony, the point of divergence for the Amesbury branch from the LSWR main line between Andover and Salisbury. The view is towards Amesbury with the respective 'up' and 'down' connections to the main line to left and right. Newton Tony Junction signal box is shown in the background. The photograph was probably taken around the time it opened in May 1904. (Author's Collection.)

A NEW BRIDGE on the Amesbury branch at Hewton Tony. The graceful curve belies the available clearance height, with evidence of recent construction showing in the freshness of the chalk cutting. (Author's Collection.)

ANOTHER NEW BRIDGE on the Amesbury line, this time on the single line connection near Newton Tony Junction. (Author's Collection.)

IN 1906 THE AMESBURY BRANCH WAS EXTENDED to Bulford and eventually Sling. Here an 0–4–4 tank waits in the siding alongside the public station. The single headcode disc is indicative of a branch working from Salisbury. (HMRS)

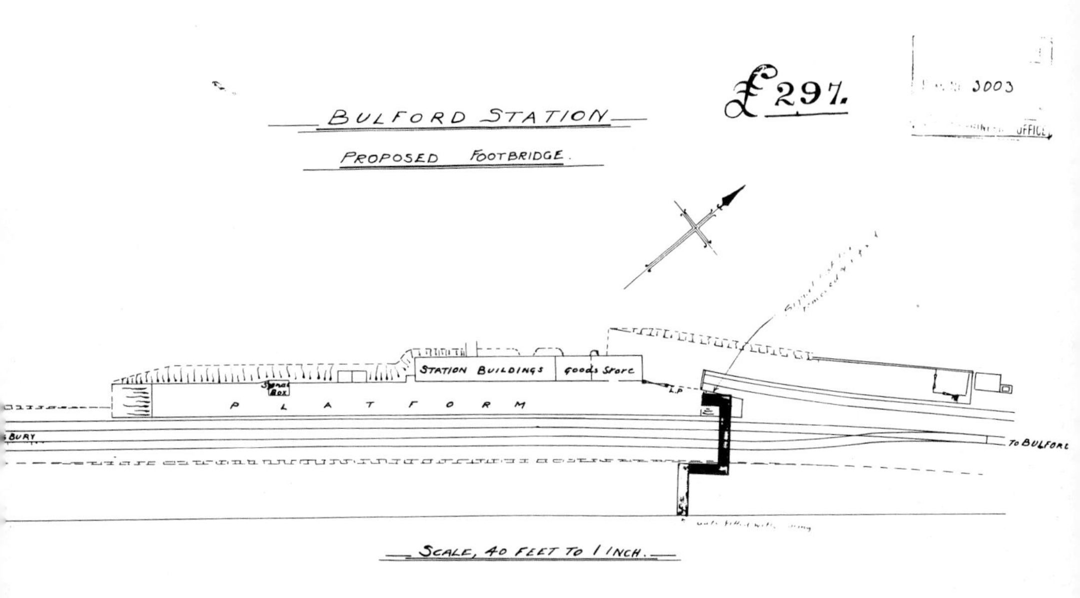

DETAILS OF THE PROPOSED FOOTBRIDGE for Bulford station in 1916, as prepared at the Eastleigh Engineer's office.

A WEST OF ENGLAND EXPRESS FROM WATERLOO. The engine is one of the Drummond 4–6–0 designs, No. 457, attached to some of what is probably the latest passenger stock. The LSWR never provided water troughs on its system and so it was the practice either to change engines at Salisbury or at least stop for water there, a legacy also of the disaster at the station when an 'up' ocean liner express left the rails due to excess speed, with considerable loss of life. The consequence of this was that it became the practice to stop all trains at the station. (Pamlin Prints.)

THE LSWR STATION AT WILTON just west of Salisbury and not far from the GWR station of the same name. Up to this point both companies' lines had run parallel with each other from Salisbury, the LSWR route continuing west towards Yeovil and Exeter whilst the GWR line swung north-west to Warminster, Westbury and eventually Bristol. Wilton was thus able to boast two stations, one on each route and totally beyond the requirements of such a small community. (Lens of Sutton.)

CONTINUING ON FROM WILTON the LSWR route passed through the minor station at Dinton before arriving at Tisbury, a small market town at which a stopping place was provided complete with the usual facilities. Here a panoramic view is obtained of both railway and town, the main station building with tile-hung façade blending in well with the other structures in the locality. (Lens of Sutton.)

BEYOND TISBURY WAS SEMLEY STATION and the last of the stopping places on the LSWR West of England route to come into the scope of this volume. In this view from the turn of the century looking towards Salisbury a line of early rolling stock, some of which appears to be oil-lit, can be seen. (Author's Collection.)

SEMLEY STATION was also intended to serve Shaftesbury, a town renowned for its steep cobbled main street as well as for a recent television commercial advertising a certain brand of brown bread. The agricultural area around the station is indicated by the milk churns on the platform, full on the left or 'up' side, with empties awaiting return to the farms on the 'down'. (Lens of Sutton.)

SLIGHTLY EARLIER THAN THE PREVIOUS SCENES is this view of Semley and, as with the companion photographs, singularly devoid of trains. The covered-in footbridge is perhaps a little unusual for a rural station and yet is a typical LSWR design. (Author's Collection.)

A FINAL VIEW OF SEMLEY, this time looking towards Yeovil. Notice in particular the LSWR livery of dark letters on a light background for the station nameboard as well as the very tall starting signal complete with its co-acting arm. The latter was provided so that it could be read easily both at a great distance and when close to. (Author's Collection.)

ALTHOUGH SLIGHTLY OUT OF THE AREA I could not resist this view of Buckhorn Tunnel west of Salisbury. The eliptical shape to the entrance was continued throughout its length and was preferred to the conventional semi-circle as it provided greater stability. (Author's Collection.)

ONE COULD HARDLY LEAVE THE AREA OF SALISBURY PLAIN without talking of the famous Stonehenge monument which had a temporary railway laid near to it during World War I. At that time though, the route was intended purely for military purposes and it was lifted with the cessation of hostilities. (Author's Collection.)

BACK TO SALISBURY AGAIN with a panoramic view of the city, once intended as a publicity photograph. Possibly the scene was used at some stage in a carriage compartment. (GWR)

WITHOUT DOUBT THE MOST FAMOUS of all the railway stations and locations in the county must be that of Swindon, 77 miles from Paddington on the main line to Bristol. In this view the station appears to be dominated by 'siphons', the code-name given to open-slatted vans whose principal purpose was to convey milk churns. Cooling was by primitive means; a rush of air through the side slats whilst the vehicle was in motion. (LGRP)

A PANORAMIC VIEW of the east end of Swindon and altered almost beyond recognition today. Apart from a veritable plethora of signal posts there is plenty of other detail to catch the eye, including a variety of 4-wheeled passenger stock, the lamp-posts and sidings full of wagons in the distance. (Lens of Sutton.)

PROBABLY TAKEN AROUND THE TURN OF THE CENTURY this superb view of the locomotive shed at Swindon shows a variety of once commonplace engine types. Up to 1900 locomotive development had been directed at Swindon by just three men, with the products of two of these, Armstrong and Dean, visible here. Notice also the baulk road and the rails laid on longitudinal timbers, held to gauge by cross timbers at set intervals. (Swindon Museum.)

PART OF THE VAST EXPANSE OF WORKSHOPS AT SWINDON which in their heyday could produce anything from a complete engine to a hand brush. Behind the factory are row upon row of cottages provided by the GWR for its employees which went by the name of Swindon village. In the foreground the large house is Newburn, the official residence of the Chief Mechanical Engineer. The property was later demolished to allow the works to expand still further. (GWR)

TAKEN SOME YEARS AFTER THE PREVIOUS VIEW the works can be seen to have expanded considerably with the carriage workshops on the left-hand side. Running from top to bottom is the main London to Bristol line whilst the Gloucester route curves away sharply to the right in the lower foreground. (GWR)

THIS TIME A VIEW FROM THE WORKS looking back towards the station. In the foreground a number of tenders are parked, presumably awaiting re-attachment to engines in the works, whilst a steam crane is also working nearby. On the Gloucester curve is an unidentified 'Star' class 4–6–0 and apparently the only engine visible. Part of the carriage and wagon works buildings can be seen to the right. (GWR)

BUILDING WORK AT SWINDON *c.* 1910. Whilst the photograph was obviously taken to show the progress of the work it is the background that holds by far the greatest interest. Notice especially the superb façade to 'A' shop, regretfully now demolished, whilst on the lines alongside the rolling-stock includes a number of steam railmotors in the overall crimson lake livery of the period. (GWR)

STEAM LASTED AT SWINDON for a number of years after the take-over by BR with this overall view giving a good impression of the various classes of engine operated by the former GWR. The family likeness is also apparent. (British Railways.)

SUNDAY, APRIL 13th

TO SWINDON WORKS

thence by coach to Avebury & Marlborough

FROM	FARES SWINDON ONLY	FARES SWINDON & ROAD TOUR	DEPART a.m.	DUE BACK p.m.
PADDINGTON	11/3	16/3	9.35	9.25
EALING BROADWAY	11/3	16/3	9.45	9.15
READING GENERAL	6/3	11/3	10.30	8.30

A PHOTOGRAPHIC COMPETITION WILL BE RUN IN CONJUNCTION WITH EACH EXCURSION

Full details from Stations, Offices and Agencies

WESTERN

REGION

FOR MANY YEARS photographic excursions such as these were a regular feature of Swindon, with a knowledgeable guide provided to conduct the visitors. A similar facility was available on most Wednesday afternoons.

BEHIND THE SCENES AT SWINDON showing the drawing office of the CME department. Here the ideas of the chief would be transferred onto paper and hopefully proven as practical proposals. Some men would spend their whole career within the department whilst others, perhaps destined for high office, merely passed through in the process of gaining experience in as many of the departments as possible. On the far wall is a GWR drop case clock, once a common feature all over the system and now a highly sought after collector's item. (GWR)

A LITTLE-KNOWN PART OF SWINDON was the chemical laboratory where a metallurgist and a number of chemists were employed. Besides their obvious duties in deciding upon the purity of metals and other substances, a number of constructional experiments were carried out whilst other work involved the use of various oils and also the effect of corrosion. In addition, water samples were sent to Swindon from most stations on the system. (GWR)

OUTSIDE THE FACTORY, the new ash-handling plant photographed on 4.8.1944. Engines arriving at Swindon for overhaul would have their fires dropped here and the char removed in buckets strung from the overhead gantry crane. (GWR)

INSIDE THE WHEELSHOP with a driving axle ready to have tyres attached. To achieve this the tyre was heated so that it expanded slightly and the wheelset was then lowered into the hot space. Cooling was achieved by natural means and would normally occupy in excess of 12 hours. (GWR)

THE LAMP ROOM STORES at Swindon Works – instant relics almost, as many of the items on display would today command a high price. (British Railways.)

AWAY FROM THE MECHANICS OF CONSTRUCTION NOW, with Armistice Day celebrated in 1938. Some of the staff from 'A' shop are gathered with their memorial wreath. A considerable number of men from the GWR served with the forces in both world wars, including volunteers from Swindon Works. (GWR)

WOMEN CLERKS AT SWINDON PROBABLY AROUND 1917. The uniform appearance of the staff is obvious and was probably the norm rather than a special effort for the camera. (GWR).

VENTURING BACK NOW TO THE EARLIEST DAYS and *North Star*, one of the first engines to be used on the GWR. Compared with the later designs that were to emerge, *North Star* can only be described as primitive and yet the family similarity is already apparent in the shape of the safety valve bonnet and copper cap to the chimney. (GWR)

FORTY YEARS LATER and the influence of William Dean is now at hand. The engine is believed to be a 4–4–0 type whilst on the right is an earlier machine temporarily minus its centre driving axle. (GWR)

THE LARGEST ENGINE EVER PRODUCED BY THE GWR AT SWINDON was Churchward's 4–6–2 *The Great Bear*. Controversy has surrounded the emergence of this solitary example of the class for many years and indeed there remain a number of unanswered questions as to its construction and use. What may not generally be known is that the engine was closer in design to a 4–8–0 as the rear set of wheels had a very limited amount of sideplay. This was one of the reasons it was restricted to a very limited route availability and spent most of its brief life working between Paddington and Bristol. (GWR)

RENUMBERED FOR USE BY THE WARTIME RAILWAY OPERATING DEPARTMENT, this former Dean Goods 0–6–0 was one of 62 engines taken over for war work and saw service in France between 1917 and 1919. After being returned to the GWR, 2349 lasted into BR days and was finally withdrawn in March 1952. (Lens of Sutton.)

AT THE TIME OF THE GROUPING OF THE RAILWAYS IN 1923, the Great Western acquired a number of smaller lines, principally in Wales. As is well known, over the years the engines from these concerns were slowly 'Westernised'. No. 1106 though is a pure GWR engine of the '1101' class which was built for the GWR in 1926 by the Avonside Engine Company principally for use in South Wales and to replace some of the earlier absorbed engines. (GWR)

MORE USUALLY ASSOCIATED WITH THE SOUTHERN RAILWAY but shown here at Swindon, WD No. 1940 is an 0–6–0T built to United States Transport Corps design. Several of these engines worked temporarily in the UK before being sent overseas from 1940 onwards. (GWR)

AT SPEED AND YET STATIONARY. A brand-new 'County' class 4–6–0 is put through its paces on the Swindon test plant deep within the works complex. For many years the mechanical affairs of Swindon were very much a closed shop as far as the other railways were concerned and yet here was a modern and well-equipped test area capable of assessing the actual output of any engine within a controlled environment. (GWR)

TOWARDS THE END OF ITS INDEPENDENT LIFE the GWR experimented with oil fuel for its engines and to this end a number of conversions were made. Shown here is a former 28xx converted to oil burning with characteristic tender tank. The view was taken by the official photographer within the Swindon works yard although the actual background has been carefully erased to prevent distraction from the subject in question. (GWR)

FRONT VIEW OF A TENDER CONVERTED TO CARRY OIL FUEL. The former shovel plate has been sealed and replaced by a simple gauge registering the amount of fuel on board. The water capacity of the tender was not affected. (GWR)

FOR MOVING LOCOMOTIVES UNDER REPAIR or other large items between the various shops an electric traverser was provided. Movement was in a north–south direction and controlled by the operator in the small wood cabin. (GWR)

THE LARGEST ITEM OF ROLLING STOCK to be built at Swindon was the solitary 'Crocodile L' capable of carrying a load of 120 tons. To provide maximum flexibility two distinct superstructures were available, with the type not shown being a set of straight girders from which a load could be slung. In the background is the drawing office complex although the area towards the Gloucester lines has been erased. (GWR)

OPPOSITE THE LOCOMOTIVE WORKS was an area designated for carriage storage, on the site of the former CME's residence. Understandably then, this shed was known as 'Newburn'. The use for the compressor has not been established. (GWR)

VICTIM OF A FIRE at an undisclosed location in late 1929. These are the remains of a former open wagon No. 109462 which was condemned at Swindon. (GWR)

ALSO ASSOCIATED WITH SWINDON were the repair shops of the road motor department where the same standards of workmanship and expertise as related to rail vehicles were applied to the road fleet. In this view a number of Thorneycroft-design vehicles, most of which appear to be of basic box van design, are shown stripped to chassis level. Of particular interest is the vehicle nearest the camera which is clearly a motor-car – possibly an official vehicle belonging to the company and used by VIPs. (GWR)

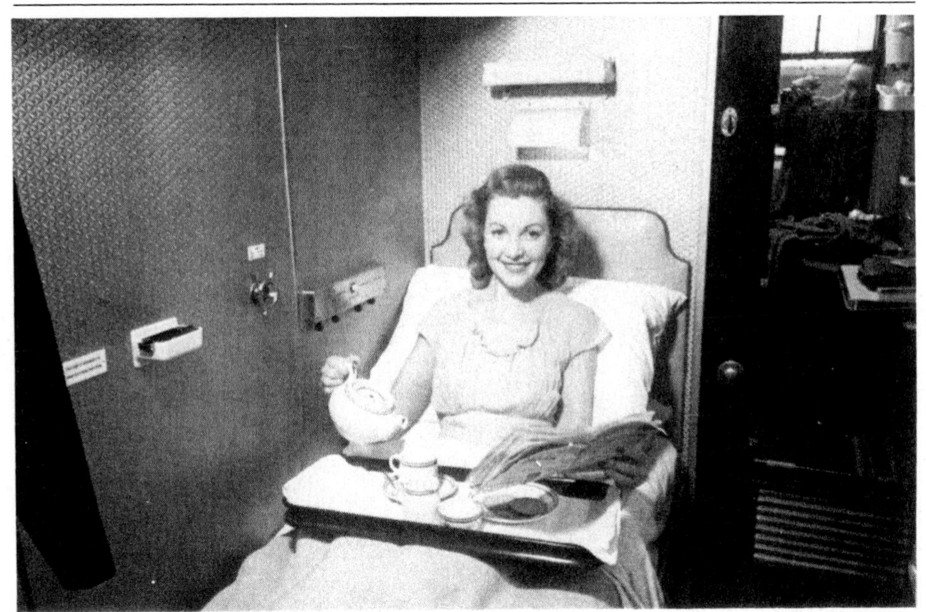

THE WORK OF THE OFFICIAL SWINDON PHOTOGRAPHERS at first hand, and a posed view to publicise a new sleeping car. The reflection of the cameraman, which would have been removed before the photograph was used in public, can be seen in the window on the right. (GWR)

ANOTHER OFFICIAL VIEW, this time part of the interior of a first class dining car. The means of air circulation is still in use today.

PART OF THE VAST ARRAY OF TIMBER in the outside timber store at Swindon in 1951. Wood was used for an infinite number of purposes within the works and often formed the major component in the building of carriages and wagons. Offcuts though, were not wasted and would be used for the making of smaller items from furniture downwards. (British Railways.)

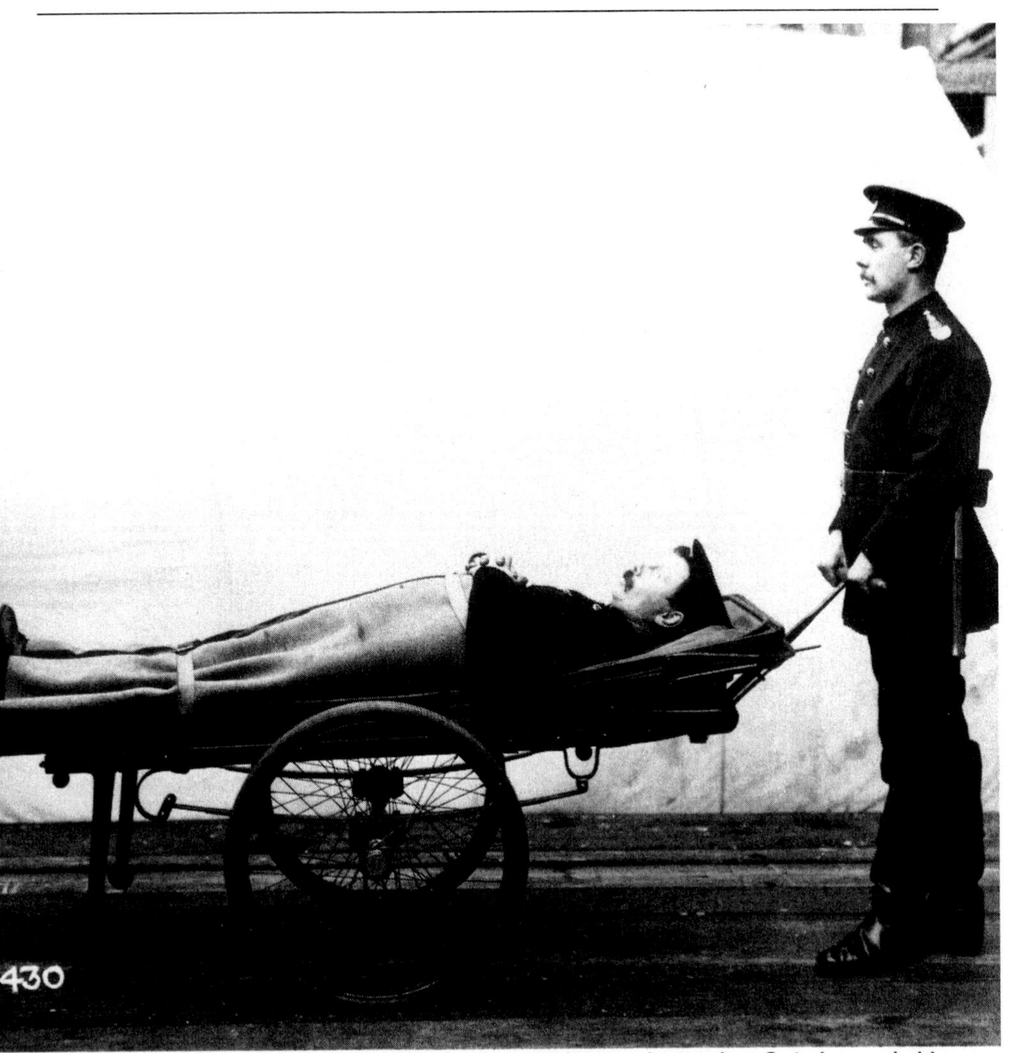

I COULD NOT RESIST THIS VIEW of the stretcher and bearer depicted at Swindon probably *c.* 1916. The sheet for the background is particularly interesting. How much use the prototype had is not certain as most stretchers were carried by two men in the more conventional manner. (GWR)

Van No. ....

GREAT WESTERN RAILWAY—GENERAL STORES, SWINDON.

RECORD OF ARTICLES EXCHANGED PER STORES VAN—YEAR 19.......... STATION

4 W.E.

1 2 3 4 1 2 3 4 1 2 3 4 1 2 3 4 1 2 3 4 1 2 3 4 1 2 3 4 1 2 3 4 1 2 3 4 1 2 3 4 1 2 3 4 1 2 3 4 1 2 3 4

Item No.	Description
122070	Glasses, L.B. Lamps 5[illegible]"×5" Flame Marked
135041	Burners, "Barton" W.O. Collars Plug [illegible]"
135049	,, "Lynlight" ,, ,, Plug [illegible]"
135036	,, "Barton" Metal Cone Plug [illegible]"
135652	,, Platform Lamp
309003	,, L.B. Signal Lamp, Disc No. 2
309008	,, ,, ,, ,, Repeater
309007	,, ,, ,, ,, Semaphore No. 1
309006	,, Route Indicator
135048	,, L.B. Stop Block Lamp
309027	Cones, L.B. Disc Lamp
309028	,, ,, Semaphore Lamp
135122	Tanks, Train Lamp
135112	Shades, Train Lamp
135088	Interiors, Stop Block Lamp
137092	Padlocks, Brass 1" for Steel B. Taps
137101	,, I.J. 2½" One Key to Differ
146012	Cocks, S.B. ¾" with Spanner
160119	Horns, Shunting No. 1
160120	,, ,, No. 3
109002	Brooms, Bass, Large
109014	,, Fibre, Platform 24"
109016	,, ,, Sweeping, 14"
109015	,, Hair, Sweeping, 14"
109019	,, Steel Wire, 12"
109012	,, Brake Van and Handles
109024	Brushes, Banister, Single
109072	,, Scrubbing, Bass
109106	,, Bass, W.C. 15"
109057	,, Oil, Round Head
109011	,, Deck, Scrubbing
109088	,, Stove, Polishing
109113	,, Whitewashing, Fibre, 8"
109114	,, 10"
159297	Sticks, Shunting, Complete
159301	,, Brake, No. 2
	WASHING
	Dusters
	Towels, Ordinary
	,, Roller
	Cloths, Sponge

12 in all Lot. 417 (37-1) 5/37 CHECKED BY

BESIDES THE MORE RENOWNED OUTPUT OF SWINDON, the works was also the location of the main stores where everything from a duster to a hand lamp could be obtained. Deliveries to outstations were on a weekly basis.

(1550)

GREAT WESTERN RAILWAY.

LOCOMOTIVE AND CARRIAGE DEPARTMENT,

SWINDON WORKS,

No. 860 10th. February, 1921

Mr. C.C.Champeney,

Mr.H.J.Bolter,

Cardiff.

Repair shoulder strap.

For Caerleon Station-master's artificial limb.

G. J. CHURCHWARD

per

To be charged to

Traffic Department. *Order No.* 860.

When the work is completed, this Order to be returned to Office of issue.

BEFORE LEAVING SWINDON I could not end this record of GWR prowess without a peep at one of the least known of all the company's activities. An artificial limb maker was indeed retained full-time on the works staff, the railway providing employment to a number of disabled men, usually injured either in wartime or as a result of an accident at work.

KNIGHTON CROSSING SIGNAL BOX on the main line between Uffington and Swindon and photographed in June 1942. This particular signal box served a dual role, protecting the adjacent road crossing as well as acting as an additional block section. It survived until November 1966 when the area was brought under the control of the new Swindon panel. (Hugh Davies.)

THE INTERIOR OF ASHBURY CROSSING SIGNAL BOX, between Uffington and Shrivenham, with signalman Sid Phillips on duty. The box here worked to Ashbury crossing on one side and Shrivenham on the other. Notice the highly polished appearance of the levers and instruments – a credit to the men, such equipment now being highly prized by collectors. (Author's Collection.)

To the Directors of
The Great Western Railway Company.

In consideration of your permitting me to walk upon your Line of Railway between 87 miles 48 chains and 88 miles 60 chains in the Parishes of Great Cheverell and Erlestoke in the County of Wilts.

I do hereby acknowledge and declare that such permission is, and shall at all times be exercised by me, upon the express condition that the Great Western Railway Company are not to be held liable, either to me or to my representatives, for any pecuniary or other responsibility, for loss of life or personal injury, or loss of or damage to property, however caused, that I may sustain in the exercise of such permission. And I do hereby undertake and agree at all times to keep the Great Western Railway Company well and effectually indemnified against all pecuniary and other responsibility, costs, damages and loss (if any) which may be incurred or sustained by them in respect of the causes aforesaid or any of them, or in any way incidental to or occasioned by the exercise of the permission hereby granted; and I do also admit and declare that the Great Western Railway Company are at liberty at any time, and from time to time, either temporarily or wholly, to withdraw such permission.

And I do further undertake and agree that in the event of their at any time or times renewing the same, then and in every such case this Agreement shall be considered as a continuing one and shall extend and apply to any and every such renewal in the same manner and with the like effect as if this Agreement were expressly entered into upon each and every such renewal.

Dated this 6th day of Nov. One thousand nine hundred and seven –

Sidney Lane
Erlestoke

Witness. Howard Bourne.
Erlestoke

ANOTHER LITTLE-KNOWN FACT CONCERNING THE GWR was that walking permits were available to bona-fide individuals. These were mainly issued to gamekeepers and others whose work involved them straying onto railway property although, as would be expected, it was at the risk of the individual concerned.

1.)

GREAT WESTERN RAILWAY.

-turn showing cause of delay to UP GOODS TRAINS at Shrivenham Station.

on Sunday day, the 18th of March 1888.

The Station Master must personally supervise the preparation of this sign it himself, and see that every train is entered which may be booked from or call at his Station which is delayed over time; and also a which may be checked or stopped out of course at his Signals or giving the fullest explanation of all delays, and he must forward the to the Divisional Superintendent as directed, in Mr. Tyrrell's No. 558, dated 21st April, 1884.

Waterlow Bros. & Layton, Limited, 24, Birchin Lane, London

Train from starting point.	Booked time at this Station.		Actual time at this Station.		Minutes lost.		Explanation of delay to be given here as per instructions above.
From.	Arr.	Dep.	Arr.	Dep.	At Signals.	At Station.	
Bristol			1.19	1.30		11	Shunted for Special [illegible] passed 1.29
Gloster	3.15	3.35	3.34	4.?		23	4 on 3.[illegible] lost Shunted for 4.30 am [illegible]
Swindon	passed 4.2						Checked local goods shunting

[illegible] Station Master. [See back for DOWN GOODS TRAINS

FOR SOME DECADES it was customary for a daily summary to be supplied from each station and junction signal box to the divisional superintendent and so account for any delays at that particular location. Separate sheets were issued for both passenger and goods trains, with 'up' and 'down' workings recorded on a particular side of the form. The incidents shown here relate to Shrivenham on 18.3.1888 and make for interesting reading.

AN EARLY BR EXPERIMENT in weed control being demonstrated at Lacock sidings in 1949. The tractor is towing a trailer loaded with concentrate and with the rails laid upon concrete pots the ride for the operator was reasonable. This particular system was not developed for main line use. (British Railways.)

CORSHAM STATION between Swindon and Bath and located on the main line to Bristol. Despite its apparent quietness at the time the photograph was taken, there was a regular clientele to and from the station. The stopping place survived until the economies of the mid-1960s. Notice especially the enamel adverts and two boys on the footbridge – obviously intent on being included in the photograph. (Lens of Sutton.)

TO COUNTERACT THE THREAT OF COMPETITION from the early road buses, the GWR built a series of halts – the word was taken from the French 'halte' – throughout the system. This one at Mill Lane Box was designed to provide for the local village and as such was served by local services, as shown here, as well as auto trains and steam railmotors. (Lens of Sutton.)

THE EPITOME OF GWR LOCOMOTIVE ENGINEERING during the last years of the nineteenth century was undoubtedly the Dean single. No. 3048 *Majestic* is shown here near Bath at the head of the 10.50 a.m. Paddington express. (GWR)

WRONG LINE WORKING at one of the tunnels west of Chippenham with the characteristic high entrance portal typical of the Brunelian architecture of the railway. (GWR)

NESTLING IN THE LEE OF THE FAMOUS BOX TUNNEL was Box station where for many years a shunting engine was retained to assist in the banking of trains up the steep incline nearby. The engine shed is visible on the left whilst the yard appears full of wagons, some no doubt from the local quarry. As an aside, the signal cabin here carried a plate reading 'Box Signal Box' whilst the station buildings were built to an early Brunel design. (Author's Collection.)

SLIGHTLY OUT OF THE AREA PERHAPS but I could not resist this exterior view of Bath station complete with its taxis and enamel adverts. The lack of other types of transport is also apparent. (GWR)

BY THE EARLY PART OF THE TWENTIETH CENTURY the influence of G.J. Churchward at Swindon was obvious. Here a brand new 'Saint' class 4–6–0, No. 177 *Robertson* is at the head of a mixed train of new and clerestory stock near Chippenham. (GWR)

AN EARLIER FORM OF TRANSPORT compared to the railway was the Kennet and Avon canal which linked London with Bristol via the rivers from which its name was derived. The waterway was later taken over by the GWR which promptly set about a slow process of diverting traffic away, allied to insufficient finance for maintenance. The inevitable result was closure. Fortunately, with the help of volunteers, the decades of decline are slowly being made good and it should not be long before the complete route is once again passable.

KENNET & AVON CANAL NAVIGATION.

WHITSUNTIDE STOPPAGE.

The **ANNUAL WHITSUNTIDE STOPPAGE** for General Repairs will commence on the **FIRST DAY** of **JUNE** Next, and terminate on the **SIXTH DAY** of **JUNE** (both days inclusive), during which time Trade will be Suspended.

W. SIMPSON,
Assistant Engineer.

ENGINEER'S OFFICE,
Bath, April 27th, 1868.

WOOTTON BASSETT STATION west of Swindon and the junction of the new line to Badminton, Bristol and South Wales which opened in 1903. The station here was in the midst of a dairy farming area and quantities of milk in churns were received for forwarding to London.

Chief Goods Manager's

GREAT WESTERN RAILWAY.

AA 10 10 87 SIX PENCE

(903)

AN AGREEMENT made the *First* **day of** *April* **One thousand, eight hundred and** ~~**eighty**~~ *ninety nine* **Between the Great Western Railway Company (hereinafter called "the Company"), by** *Charles Abraham Roberts* **their District Goods Manager, of the one part, and** *Sydney Charles Burt of 36 St John's Road Clifton, Bristol* **(hereinafter called "the Agent") of the other part.**

1. The said *Sydney Charles Burt* hereby agrees to become Carting-Agent to the Company for the Station and District of *Wootton Bassett* and the Company agrees to employ the said *Sydney Charles Burt* as Carting-Agent on the following conditions:—

2. The said Agent hereby undertakes to find, in sufficient quantities, all requisite and suitable Stock in Vans, Carts, Trollies, Timber Carriages, Horses, Harness, Pulleys, Ropes, and other necessary appliances; to employ proper, civil, energetic, and trustworthy Men, to the satisfaction of the Company, for the collection of Goods and Merchandise within the said District, and for the delivery thereof to or from the said Station, and to remove such Men, Horses, or Vehicles, as may from time to time be considered by or on behalf of the Company to be objectionable or unsuitable.

3. The said Agent, as and when required, shall and will provide a suitable and convenient Office or Receiving House, and shall have painted in a bold and legible manner in some public and conspicuous part thereof the words "Great Western Railway Company," "*S. C. Burt* Agent," and shall also have the same words legibly painted on the sides or fixed Covers of all Vehicles used or kept under or in pursuance of this Agreement.

4. Within the Free Cartage District hereinafter specified the said Agent is not to make or collect any additional charge for Collection, Delivery, Booking, or other service, over and above the Company's charges on the Goods entrusted to him, when invoiced or to be charged at "Carted" rates, except as may be herein provided for.

5. The Free Cartage District for the *Town* of *Wootton Bassett* shall extend from the Station *two miles in any direction*

TO CATER FOR THE COLLECTION AND DELIVERY OF PARCELS, the GWR developed a network of local carriers with one retained at most stations. Understandably, before an individual would be entrusted with the cartage arrangements an agreement was drawn up to protect the interests of the railway. Such arrangements lasted until the advent of the country lorry service from the mid-1920s onwards.

BRINKWORTH STATION on the new South Wales direct main line. The station here served the village of the same name which was situated just out of camera to the right. The tall home signal was positioned so that its indication could be seen above the bridge from which the photograph was taken. (LGRP)

ALDERTON TUNNEL, again on the new line. This took the route under the land of one particular man who otherwise objected to the passage of the new railway. In this view the cutting sides have yet to gain a growth of vegetation which nowadays extends almost to rail level.

The Wilts, Somerset & Weymouth Railway Compy

CERTIFICATE OF £50 SHARE.

This is to Certify that Thomas George Wilmer of Yeovil Clerk is the Proprietor of the SHARE No 1550 of the WILTS, SOMERSET AND WEYMOUTH RAILWAY COMPANY, subject to the Rules Orders and Regulations of the said Company.

Given under their Common Seal the Eighth day of October in the year of our Lord 1845.

Registered. No [illegible]

ONE OF THE MOST IMPORTANT BRANCHES from the original GWR was the Wilts, Somerset & Weymouth company whose line ran from Bath through Trowbridge to Westbury and thence via Castle Cary to Yeovil and Weymouth. (A further branch was later provided from Westbury to Salisbury which is referred to later in the book). The certificate illustrated was one of a number that have survived from the old company with the original now in the keeping of British Railways archives.

Bath and Weymouth
Great Western Union Railway,

Viâ FROME, WINCANTON, STALBRIDGE, CERNE ABBAS, and DORCHESTER; with Lines of Communication from the SOMERSETSHIRE COLLIERIES to BRADFORD, TROWBRIDGE, WESTBURY, WARMINSTER, and FROME.

Capital, £1,000,000, in 10,000 Shares of £100 each.

Deposit, £2 10s. per Share.

NO FURTHER CALL OR LIABILITY UNTIL THE ACT OF INCORPORATION IS OBTAINED.

Provisional Committee:

SIR JOHN SMYTH, BART.
SIR FREDERICK GEORGE JOHNSTONE, BART.
THE HON. W. F. S. PONSONBY, M.P.
WILLIAM MILES, ESQ., M.P.
THOMAS FOWELL BUXTON ESQ., M.P.
W. WARTON BURDON, ESQ., M.P.
THOMAS SHEWELL BAILWARD, ESQ.
H. K. M. BROOKE, ESQ.
JAMES BOWER, ESQ.
RICHARD BOWER, ESQ.
EDWARD FRANCIS COLSTON, ESQ.
JOHN CREE, ESQ.
CHAS. CURME, ESQ.
JOHN COX, ESQ.
WM. DEVENISH, ESQ.
WM. ELIOT, ESQ.
JAMES FUSSELL, ESQ.
BENJAMIN GREY, ESQ.
ROBERT HAYNES, ESQ.
MR. THOMAS HOLWEY
VAUGHAN JENKINS, ESQ.
W. COXETER JAMES, ESQ.
CHARLES LOWDER, ESQ.
MR. WM. LOCK
CHARLES AUGUSTUS MANNNIG, ESQ.
WILLIAM MATRAVERS, ESQ.
HENRY MANT, ESQ.
URIAH MESSITER, ESQ.
JOHNSON PHILLOTT, ESQ.
MR. SAMUEL PROVIS
CAPT. SAVAGE
GEORGE SHEPPARD, ESQ.
T. B. SAUNDERS, ESQ.
CAPT. SCOBELL, R. N.
MR. G. P. SCOTT
MR. JAMES TAYLER SINGER
GEO. TAYLOR, ESQ., M.D.
HYDE SALMON WHALLEY, ESQ.
G. C. WELSFORD, ESQ.
JAMES ANTHONY WICKHAM, ESQ.
MR. F. WITHERS
F. BOUCHER WRIGHT, ESQ.
REV. H. F. YEATMAN
FRANCIS YERBURY, ESQ.

With power to add to their number.

BANKERS:

MESSRS. JONES, LOYD, & CO. } *London.*
MESSRS. WILLIAMS, DEACON, & CO. } *London.*
MESSRS. HOBHOUSE, PHILLOTT, & LOWDER .... *Bath.*
WEST OF ENGLAND AND SOUTH WALES BANKING COMPANY .... *Bristol,*
WILLIAM ELIOT, ESQ., AND MESSRS. WILLIAMS, COX, & CO. .... *Dorchester and Weymouth.*

ENGINEERS:

MESSRS. HOPKINS & SONS.

SOLICITORS:

MESSRS. MANT & BRUCE, *Bath*—MR. W. B. SCOTT, *Weymouth.*

SECRETARY:

MR. T. S. SCRIVEN, *Weymouth.*

PROSPECTUS DETAILS for the ill-fated Bath and Weymouth, Great Western Union Railway. The information and map for this proposed line on the following pages makes for interesting scrutiny especially in view of the actual railways later built in the area.

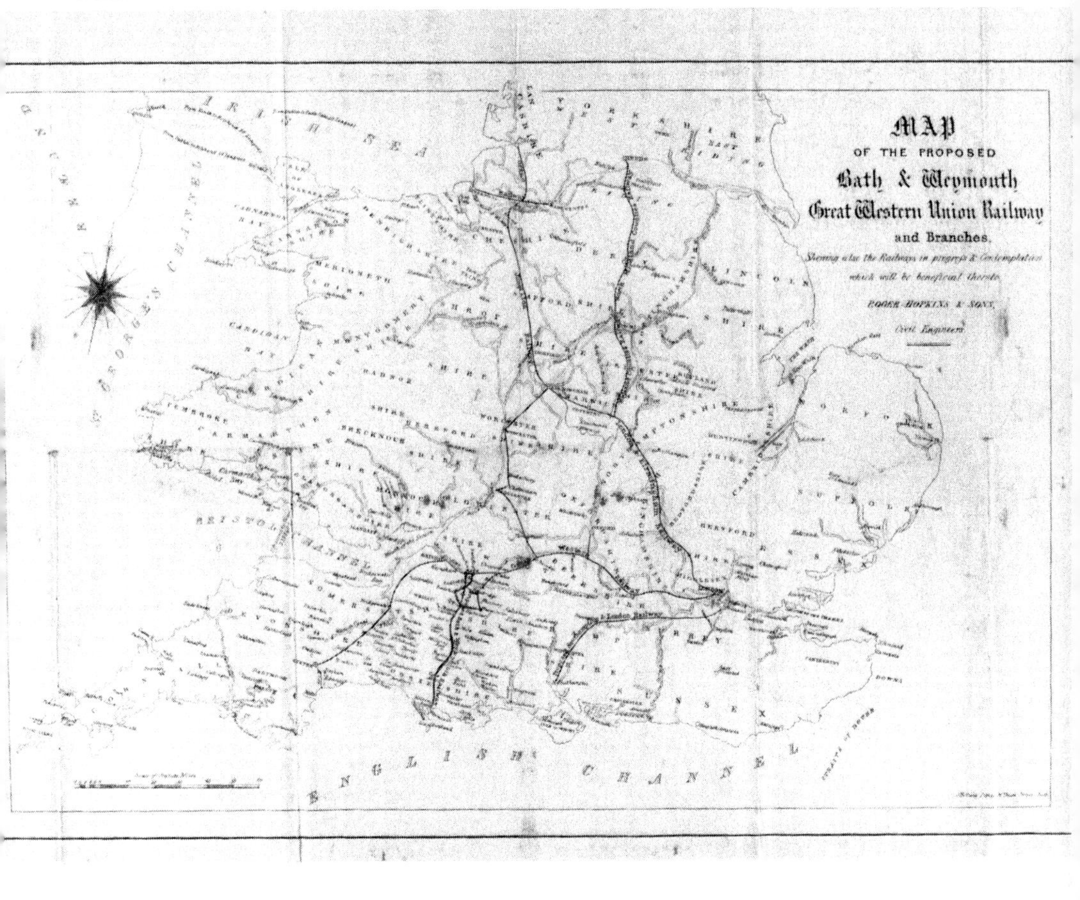
MAP
OF THE PROPOSED
Bath & Weymouth
Great Western Union Railway
and Branches.
Shewing also the Railways in progress & Contemplation
which will be beneficial thereto.
ROGER HOPKINS & SONS,
Civil Engineers
IRISH SEA
ST GEORGES CHANNEL
BRISTOL CHANNEL
ENGLISH CHANNEL

GREAT WESTERN RAILWAY

Particulars of Shed and other accommodation fo

ENGINE SHED (*Sketch Plan to be attached*).

How built (Stone, Brick or Wood)		Brick
Inside dimensions.	Length	100 0
	Breadth	39 0
	Height to top of roof ridge ...	28 6
	Do. do. wall plate	15 0
	Cubical contents ...	
Style of Roof (Gable, Hip Gable or Saw-tooth)		Gable
Roof principals (Material)		Iron
If fitted with Smoke Troughs ...		Yes
Date built, or date Shed was first used ...		
Length of each Line used for running Engines		94 0
Do. do. do. repairs ...		None
Engine Pits—length of each used for running Engines		88 0
Do. do. do. repairs ...		None

SHOPS OR OFFICES OUTSIDE THE SHED.

		Foreman	Clerks	Stores	Fitting Shop	Stores	Stores	Enmen	Stores
How built (Stone, Brick or Wood) ...		Brick	Brick	Brick	Brick	Wood	Iron	Wood	
Inside dimensions.	Length	12 0	16 6	12 5	23 4	14 0	9 6	24 6	30 0
	Breadth	11 4	12 0	12 0	15 0	8 0	8 0	7 0	7 0
	Height to top of roof ridge	14 0	14 0	14 0	16 6	7 9	8 6	7 8	7 8
	Do. do. wall plate	10 0	10 0	10 0	12 0	Old Horse Box	6 0	Old Coaches	Old Coaches
	Cubical contents								
Style of Roof (Gable, Hip Gable or Saw-tooth)			Lean to	Lean to	Lean to		Gable		
Roof principals (Material)		Wood	Wood	Wood	Wood		Corr. Iron		
Date built, or date opened									

Length of Line used for repairs ... 120 0

Do. Engine Pit used for repairs ... 11 0

EACH GWR LOCOMOTIVE SHED was originally provided with an entry in a register of facilities maintained by the locomotive department. Besides the previous sheet of dimensions there was also a sketch plan of the type shown here which provides a useful amount of information on the facilities which existed prior to the shed's closure in 1923.

COMOTIVE DEPARTMENT.

g Engines at Trowbridge Station.

UTSIDE SHED.

Lines available for standing Engines ... See tracing

Engine Pits—length of each ... 100 0 40 0 40 0 at Coal Stage.

Do. at Station ... 32 0

NGINE TURNTABLES.

Diameter ... ... 45 0 ~~extension bars~~ No extension bars 1908

Length of Rail 44 10

Girders (Material) ... Iron

How turned ... ... Hand gear

Where fixed ... ... Near Shed 500 ft W of Shed measured along Coal Stage road.

Date fixed ... ...

Maker ... ... G W R Co

OAL STAGE.

Sketch and size ... ...

Engine Shed closed 2/6/23.

Number of Cranes or Tips ... One crane

How built (Stone, Brick or Wood) Wood

Date built ... ...

AND FURNACE.

Outside dimensions 13 0 length, 6 6 breadth, 10 6 x 9 6 height

Brief description and Sketch Brick & iron built

Date built ...

Where situated ... Near Shed

Date Certified 10 1 99 ______ Superintendent's Signature.

" " 3 04 H Simpson per EWM " "

" " " "

" " " "

" " " "

" " " "

Prospectus.

The immense advantages of the Railway System of Communication being now more fully appreciated than at any former period, in consequence of its speed, safety, and economy, Companies have been recently formed, or prospectuses issued for constructing nearly 1500 Miles of Railways in various parts of the Kingdom. It therefore behoves all those Agricultural, Manufacturing, and Commercial Classes who enjoy not these benefits, forthwith to seek them on the principle of self-preservation. Among several others the Act for the Great Western Railway was passed during the last Session of Parliament, and it is confidently expected, that in less than five years, the whole Line of Railway from London to Bristol will be completed; and in two years, from Bath to Bristol. The necessity of Lines of Railways, diverging in various directions from this Main Line, is daily becoming more apparent, and arrangements are therefore in progress in several places with that view. The propriety of a Railway from Bath to Weymouth, uniting with the Great Western Railway at Bath, and also at Bathford, is now submitted to the notice of the Public, in the confident expectation, that in a very short time, the whole of the Capital necessary for that purpose will be subscribed.

These Lines of Railway, which will be about 102 Miles in length, (40 of which will be double, the remainder single,) is intended to pass through the important Manufacturing Town of Frome, and the Market Town of Wincanton, near Bruton, and through or near Stalbridge, Cerne-Abbas, and Dorchester, with Lines of Communication from the Somersetshire Coal Fields at Radstock, and other places, one joining the Main Line at Frome, and proceeding from thence to Warminster; the other joining the Main Line at or near Monkton Combe, and diverging out of it at Freshford, passing near the important Manufacturing Towns of Bradford, Trowbridge, and Westbury, and joining the Line leading from Frome to Warminster, near the latter place. The Country in general, is exceedingly favorable for a Railway, and the estimated expense is therefore much less than those of many similar Undertakings.

The advantages of this Railway are too numerous to be fully detailed in a Prospectus. It will open a cheap and expeditious communication between London and Weymouth, *viâ* the Great Western Railway, saving Passengers nearly six hours in time; it will connect the centre of the British with the Bristol Channel; it will afford a cheap and abundant supply of Coals from the Somersetshire Collieries at the one end, and the Port of Weymouth at the other end, to a very extensive and populous district, and to important Clothing and other Manufacturing Establishments, which now obtain fuel at considerable expense; it will convey Culm and small Coal, for burning Lime for Agricultural and Building purposes, much cheaper than it can be procured by any other means, and the District itself abounds with Limestone; it will provide new markets for the Agricultural produce of the District, and effect a considerable saving in their carriage; Cloth, Hardware, and other manufactured goods, will be taken from the Manufacturing Districts of Somersetshire and Wiltshire to London, Bristol, Liverpool and their other respective destinations, and general merchandise from Bristol; the Clothing Districts will be supplied with Wool and other raw materials, as well as Coal, as before mentioned; the valuable Stone raised in the island of Portland, and the Paving Stone from Purbeck, as well as the fine Freestone from Bath, and in other parts of the Line, will be conveyed into the interior of the Country for various buildings; and Timber, Slate, Fish, and other commodities, from both ends of the line, will be transmitted for general consumption. There is also Iron Stone under the Mendip Hills, near the proposed Line of Railway.

Weymouth, which is the proposed Southern Terminus of the Line, is well known as a fashionable Watering Place, and an important Post-Office Packet Station to and from Guernsey and Jersey, which is in the direct route to the South of France; many Foreign Vessels also frequently land Mails and Passengers; and there is too a Shipping Trade, which may be considerably augmented, as the Harbour is very commodious, and capable of great improvement and extension, and Ships of any burden may anchor in Portland Roads. A Bridge is about to be erected from Portland to the main land, an Act of Parliament, authorising its construction, having been obtained during the last Session. There are, at the present time, three Post-Office Steam Packets employed between Weymouth and the Channel Islands, the expense of which is more than defrayed (and a considerable revenue obtained) by the large number of Passengers continually conveyed. There are also Steam Packets from Jersey to St. Malo; but it is in contemplation to establish a direct Post-Office Steam Packet communication between Weymouth and St. Malo, by which this would become the most elegible route from nearly all parts of the Kingdom to the South of France. There is, too, a constant influx of visitors to Weymouth during both Summer and Winter. No one capable of forming an opinion can for a moment doubt that their numbers would be considerably enhanced by the facility of communication which Railways could afford.

In addition to the Towns which have been already mentioned as lying in the direct Line of the Railway, the following Towns being in the vicinity, would also be materially benefited, as well as the Agriculturalists of the District generally; *viz.* Chippenham, Melksham, Shepton-Mallet, Castle-Carey, Shaftesbury, Milborne-Port, Sherborne, Yeovil, Ilchester, South Petherton, Crewkerne, Sturminster-Newton, Blandford-Forum, Beaminster, Beer-Regis, Charmouth, Lyme-Regis, Bridport, Abbotsbury, &c. It also will materially increase the traffic of the Great Western and other Railways, and thus add to the value and utility of all, from whence this Railway will receive reciprocal advantages. A Line has been surveyed from the Great Western Railway to Cheltenham and Gloucester, and from Gloucester to Birmingham, the Plans of which have been duly lodged, and Notice given preparatory to applications to Parliament in this present Session; and a Railway is now making from Birmingham to Liverpool.

There will then be continuous communications not only from Weymouth to London, Bath, and Bristol, but also to Birmingham, Liverpool, Manchester, Sheffield, Leeds, and various other places, and the Inhabitants of the important Districts adjoining these numerous Railways will then avail themselves of the opportunity of visiting Weymouth, the distance being less from Birmingham to Weymouth, than to Brighton.

Travellers will also pass from the South of Ireland through Bristol and Weymouth to the Channel Islands, and the South of France, as well as from Liverpool and other parts of the North of England. The Revenue of this Railway will not however depend merely on Passengers, although that will amount to a very large sum per annum; but it will be both a Commercial and an Agricultural Railway, (as has already been pointed out,) and thus supply the wants and meet the desires of a very numerous and increasing pupulation.

WESTBURY NORTH SIGNAL BOX which controlled the junction of the former Wilts, Somerset and Weymouth line with the connection to the line from Reading. As the name implies the 'box was situated at the north of the station and was opened by the GWR in 1899. It remained basically unaltered until closure in 1984 and was one of the last remaining mechanical 'boxes on the Western Region to be worked by two men. (GWR)

THE SOUTH END OF THE STATION AT WESTBURY *c.* 1900 with a variety of early stock in view. Behind the trains is the Westbury Iron Works which maintained its own private siding. A considerable amount of traffic was generated for the railway from this source. (Lens of Sutton.)

A FINAL VIEW OF WESTBURY in the days when most goods was transported by rail – as judged by the full sidings of wagons. Notice also the red distant arms to the signals. This was the usual colour until 1927 when a change was made to the now standard yellow. (Lens of Sutton.)

10 & 11 VICTORIÆ.——Sess. 1847.

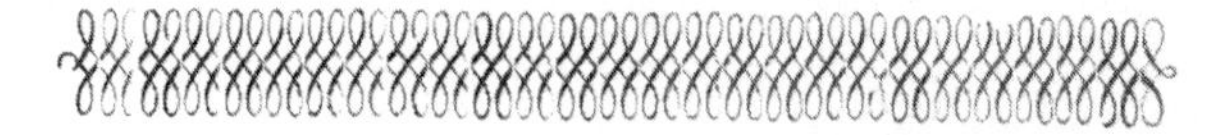

A

BILL

For making a Railway from the BERKS and HANTS RAILWAY at HUNGERFORD, to join the Line of the WILTS, SOMERSET, and WEYMOUTH RAILWAY at WESTBURY and DEVIZES.

[*Note.*—The Words printed in *Italics* are proposed to be inserted in Committee.]

WHEREAS an Act was passed in the Fifth Year of the Reign of His Majesty King William the Fourth, intituled, "An Act for making a Railway from Bristol to join "the London and Birmingham Railway near London, to be "called the 'Great Western Railway,' with Branches there- "from to the Towns of Bradford and Trowbridge, in the County "of Wilts," whereby several Persons were incorporated by the Name and Style of the "Great Western Railway Company":

Preamble.
5 Will. 4, c. 107.

And whereas the Provisions of the said Act were Amended and Enlarged by several subsequent Acts, passed respectively in the Sixth Year of the Reign of His said Majesty, and in the First, the Second, and Seventh and Ninth Years of the Reign of Her present Majesty Queen VICTORIA:

6 Will. 4, c. 38.
1 Vic. c. 91.
1 Vic. Sess. 2, c. 92.
2 Vic. c. 27.
7 Vic. c. 3.
9 Vic. c. 14.

And whereas an Act was passed in the Eighth Year of the Reign of Her present Majesty, intituled, "An Act for making a

18. A "Railway

ANOTHER MAIN LINE running through Wiltshire on an east to west basis was the Berks and Hants Extension route, not to be confused because of the company's name! Basically it was an extension of the erstwhile Berks and Hants railway from Hungerford through to Devizes and although first mooted in 1847 the line was not fully opened until November 1862.

FIRST OF THE STATIONS on the B & H Extension was at Bedwyn, now the terminus of the diesel shuttle from Reading. (The main line still continues west of this point although not served by a local service.) Of immediate interest is the number of persons present, most of whom would appear to be railway employees. The station architecture was also unique to the line and will be seen elsewhere in this book. (Author's Collection.)

THE BERKS AND HANTS EXTENSION ROUTE carried the line westwards through the Vale of Pewsey where a station was situated to serve the village of the same name. Indeed it is still open today although it now acts as a railhead to replace those other stopping places long since closed. (Lens of Sutton.)

THIS TIME A CLOSE-UP VIEW of Pewsey with the non-standard GWR footbridge in evidence. Originally, much of the B & H Extension line was single track with passing loops at the various stations but it was upgraded by the GWR from the late 1880s onwards and so formed part of the new main line to the west avoiding Bristol. (Lens of Sutton.)

GREAT WESTERN RAILWAY

(903)

AN AGREEMENT made the *17th* day of *December* One thousand *Nine hundred & Twentyone.*

Between the Great Western Railway Company (hereinafter called "the Company"), by *William Harry Lucas*

their District Goods Manager, of the one part, and *George William Plank of Pewsey Wilts*

(hereinafter called "the Agent") of the other part.

1. The said *George William Plank* hereby agrees to become Carting-Agent to the Company for the Station and District of *Pewsey* and the Company agrees to employ the said *George William Plank* as Carting-Agent on the following conditions:—

2. The said Agent hereby undertakes to find, in sufficient quantities, all requisite and suitable Stock in Vans, Carts, Trolleys, Timber Carriages, Horses, Harness, Pulleys, Ropes, and other necessary appliances; to employ proper, civil, energetic, and trustworthy Men, to the satisfaction of the Company, for the collection of Goods and Merchandise within the said District, and for the delivery thereof to or from the said Station, and to remove such Men, Horses, or Vehicles, as may from time to time be considered by or on behalf of the Company to be objectionable or unsuitable.

3. The said Agent, as and when required, shall and will provide a suitable and convenient Office or Receiving House, and shall have painted in a bold and legible manner in some public and conspicuous part thereof the words "Great Western Railway Company," " *G W Plank* Agent," and shall also have the same words legibly painted on the sides or fixed covers of all Vehicles used or kept under or in pursuance of this Agreement.

4. Within the Free Cartage District hereinafter specified the said Agent is not to make or collect any additional charge for Collection, Delivery, Booking, or other service, over and above the Company's charges on the Goods entrusted to him, when invoiced or to be charged at "Carted" rates, except as may be herein provided for.

5. The Free Cartage District for the *district* of *Pewsey* shall extend from the Station *for a distance of one mile therefrom by any public road —*

CARTAGE AGREEMENT FOR PEWSEY.

ONLY TWO HALTS WERE PROVIDED along the whole of the line from Hungerford to Devizes, at Manningford, as seen here, and at Wootton Rivers. Both served sparsely populated areas and had a comparatively short life of around thirty years. (Lens of Sutton.)

Halt, Wootton Rivers

AN EARLY VIEW OF THE OTHER HALT at Wootton Rivers west of Savernake. Notice the staggered platforms which were by no means unique at this type of stopping place. Only basic facilities are provided, a waiting shed and little else, pre-empting the changes to be brought about at many much larger stations in later years. (Lens of Sutton.)

THE DELIGHTFULLY-NAMED WOODBOROUGH STATION again with a main building to typical B & H company design. As with the other stopping places along the route the resources for passengers and goods were similar except that here an extra shed has been added on the platform at some stage, probably for parcels traffic. (Lens of Sutton.)

AN EVOCATIVE PHOTOGRAPH of the station and permanent way staff outside Woodborough signal box, probably *c.* 1900. The 'T' and 'S' plates stood for 'Telegraph' and 'Signals' and were used to indicate if the assistance of men from these particular departments was required. (Jack Carpenter Collection.)

A FURTHER UPGRADING OF FACILITIES on the line took place in the 1940s as witness here in the rebuilding of an overbridge near Woodborough. Notice the 'ATC' ramp in the forground laid at a slight angle to the running rails so as to even out wear on the engine pick-up shoe. (GWR)

FOR MANY YEARS the most important of all the stations on the line was at Patney & Chirton. Here the original Berks and Hants turned north-west towards Devizes whilst the GWR later built a new line to Westbury as part of its upgrading of facilities to the west. Not confirmed is the fact that the buildings seen in the photograph were erected at the time the cut-off was provided. Although now long demolished, a similar structure which dates from the same period survives at Bramley (Hants) on the line between Basingstoke and Reading. (Lens of Sutton.)

FOR MANY YEARS an amount of military traffic was handled at Patney owing to the proximity of the station to the fringes of Salisbury Plain. A special military platform was also provided and found much use, such as shown here in 1910 with the Manchester Regiment detraining. (Lens of Sutton.)

TWO STATIONS WERE BUILT ON THE STERT AND WESTBURY LINE from Patney to Westbury. This is the second, at Lavington, although it must be said that neither attracted much in the way of rail traffic. In the station on this occasion is a mixed goods train, apparently in the course of shunting vehicles on the 'up' line. (Lens of Sutton.)

A DELIGHTFUL VIEW OF LAVINGTON, probably *c.* 1910, this time with a mixed rake of passenger stock painted in the GWR crimson lake livery of the period. Included in the line is one of the new 'Toplight' vehicles which were some of the first to dispense with the traditional roof clerestory. Notice also the timber platform which was a fairly common feature, used as a means of economy where little weight needed to be supported. (Lens of Sutton.)

RETURNING NOW TO THE FINAL SECTION OF THE BERKS AND HANTS ROUTE seen here on the approach to Devizes via the tunnel immediately preceding the station. An indication is also gained of the single track status of much of the original line although sufficient land had been purchased for doubling, even though north-west of Patney this was never carrried out. (J. Roberts Collection.)

THE RAILWAY EMERGED FROM THE TUNNEL immediately into the station and yard area which was unfortunately situated some little distance from the town. Despite this disadvantage there was plenty of space available for railway use as indicated here with a siding running some distance away from the main line and at right angles to it. (J. Roberts Collection.)

A CHARMING VIEW OF DEVIZES STATION at the time when the baulk 'road' remained as well as the overall roof. Today such a photograph appears extremely dated and yet it was probably taken sometime in the early years of the present century. Access to the station was via the road visible on the right which led down from the delightful-sounding Monday Market Street. (Lens of Sutton.)

NORTH OF DEVIZES the single line continued towards Holt Junction and again with sufficient room available for a double line of rails if required. This view is of Pans Lane Halt just north of Devizes which attracted little passenger patronage although quantities of milk were handled. (Lens of Sutton.)

THE LINE FROM DEVIZES joined the original branch from Chippenham to Trowbridge at the junction station at Holt which faced towards Westbury. For many years the line through Devizes was also able to serve as a useful diversionary route for trains from both the West Country and Bristol whilst a number of services were also regularly diverted in this manner to ensure the locomotive crews remained familiar with the line. (Lens of Sutton.)

AWAY FROM THE BERKS AND HANTS NOW and instead we return to the Salisbury branch of the Wilts, Somerset & Weymouth from Westbury. This was for many years – and indeed still is – a through artery between Bristol and the south coast. SR No. 1626 at the head of a train of GWR stock near Warminster on 18.6.1936. (W. Vaughan Jenkins.)

WISHFORD STATION, with the station master evidently more interested in the photographer than the approaching train. The station buildings here portray an architectural style belonging to two distinct periods. That on the right is the original building, the small waiting shelter opposite being provided some years later when the line was doubled. (Lens of Sutton.)

WYLYE, pronounced 'Why-lee', on the same line to Salisbury. Here the broad gauge origins of the railway show up well, with the wide expanse of the entrance to the goods shed far larger than needed for the wagons in view. The train would appear to be formed of 4-wheeled passenger stock although at the rear are attached two short horse boxes. (Lens of Sutton.)

APART FROM WARMINSTER the busiest station on the line was probably that at Codford from which a branch led off to a railway encampment on Salisbury Plain. This view though, mainly depicts the superb signal box with the signalmen, station master and probably porters posed for the photographer. (Author's Collection.)

DESPITE THE APPARENT LACK OF MOVEMENT in this view of Codford there is plenty of action behind the scenes. In the cattle dock for example there are a number of vehicles whilst the yard sports a variety of sacks, churns and barrels. (Lens of Sutton.)

WHAT IS NOW THE A36 MAIN ROAD THROUGH CODFORD VILLAGE, although at the time the photograph was taken, *c.* 1916, it was little more than a rutted track. The buildings on either side of the road are in connection with the military encampments of the area and it would appear that there are several short lengths of railway track upside-down on the right-hand bank. (Author's collection.)

RAILWAY CAMP NO. 6 AT CODFORD, World War One, with the rail connection provided from the GWR station of the same name. The trackwork can be seen to be lightly laid although quite substantial compared with that in the next view. (Lens of Sutton.)

A FINAL VIEW OF CODFORD CAMP and this time with trackwork that is anything but permanent. Besides the railway connection here another short-lived line led off to Sutton Veney with a number of the main-line stations on the perimeters of the area dealing with vast amounts of traffic around this time. (Author's Collection.)

MOST IMPORTANT OF THE STATIONS on the Salisbury branch was at Warminster shown here still with its overall roof. For many years a banking engine was based here and used to bank trains up to the station on the steep climb from Westbury. (Lens of Sutton.)

A SOMEWHAT HEAVILY RETOUCHED CARD, although still basically accurate, of the little terminus at Calne on the branch from Chippenham. From here the GWR operated a bus service to Marlborough via Avebury whilst the station itself dealt with large quantities of meat products from the factory of Messrs Harris. (Lens of Sutton.)

Chief Goods Manager's

GREAT WESTERN RAILWAY.

(903)

AN AGREEMENT made the *First* day of *April* One thousand, eight hundred and ~~eighty~~ *ninety-nine* Between the Great Western Railway Company (hereinafter called "the Company"), by *Charles Abraham Roberts* their District Goods Manager, of the one part, and *Sydney Charles Burt of 32 St John's Road, Clifton, Bristol* (hereinafter called "the Agent") of the other part.

1. The said *Sydney Charles Burt* hereby agrees to become Carting-Agent to the Company for the Station and District of *Calne* and the Company agrees to employ the said *Sydney Charles Burt* as Carting-Agent on the following conditions:—

2. The said Agent hereby undertakes to find, in sufficient quantities, all requisite and suitable Stock in Vans, Carts, Trollies, Timber Carriages, Horses, Harness, Pulleys, Ropes, and other necessary appliances; to employ proper, civil, energetic, and trustworthy Men, to the satisfaction of the Company, for the collection of Goods and Merchandise within the said District, and for the delivery thereof to or from the said Station, and to remove such Men, Horses, or Vehicles, as may from time to time be considered by or on behalf of the Company to be objectionable or unsuitable.

3. The said Agent, as and when required, shall and will provide a suitable and convenient Office or Receiving House, and shall have painted in a bold and legible manner in some public and conspicuous part thereof the words "Great Western Railway Company," "*S. C. Burt* Agent," and shall also have the same words legibly painted on the sides or fixed Covers of all Vehicles used or kept under or in pursuance of this Agreement.

4. Within the Free Cartage District hereinafter specified the said Agent is not to make or collect any additional charge for Collection, Delivery, Booking, or other service, over and above the Company's charges on the Goods entrusted to him, when invoiced or to be charged at "Carted" rates, except as may be herein provided for.

5. The Free Cartage District for the *Town and District* of *Calne* shall extend from the Station *to any distance within a radius of one mile from the station within Gates — if Gates are passed the tolls are chargeable to the Public*

THERE WERE TWO HALTS ON THE CALNE BRANCH; this one at Stanley Bridge opened prior to 1923 with a conventional pagoda shelter standing on a timber and ash platform. The pagoda design was of course Chinese in origin although what may not be so widely known is that the word itself has origins in the Portuguese language. (Lens of Sutton.)

THE SECOND STOPPING PLACE ON THE BRANCH was at the delightfully-named Black Dog Halt, a little way short of the actual terminus. This was a private stopping place intended to serve a private estate and so for many years it did not appear in the public timetable. Alongside the platform was a siding, the entrance to which was controlled from a ground frame, primarily used for coal and other goods destined for the stately home nearby. (Lens of Sutton.)

MALMESBURY RAILWAY.

CAPITAL £60,000, IN 6,000 SHARES OF £10 EACH.

DEPOSIT 10s. PER SHARE, TO BE PAID ON APPLICATION.

PROVISIONAL COMMITTEE.

THOMAS DANIEL HILL, Esq., 30, Grosvenor Place, and 4, Mincing Lane, London, *Chairman.*
SIR RICHARD HUNGERFORD POLLEN, Bart., Rodbourne, Malmesbury.
CHARLES WILLIAM MILES, Esq., Burton Hill, Malmesbury.
WALTER POWELL, Esq., M.P., Dauntsey House, Malmesbury.
WILLIAM HOLLIS LUCE, Esq., Burton Hill, Malmesbury.
CHARLES RICHARD LUCE, Esq., Halcombes, Malmesbury.
WILLIAM PANTING, Esq., Auctioneer and Estate Agent, Malmesbury.

BANKERS.

THE WILTS AND DORSET BANK, Malmesbury.

ENGINEER.

R. J. WARD, 11, Great Queen Street, Westminster.

SOLICITORS.

JONES & FORRESTER, Malmesbury.

SECRETARY.

CHARLES F. HART (Berks and Hants Extension Railway), Devizes.

PROSPECTUS.

The Malmesbury Railway Company is intended to be incorporated for the purpose of constructing a Railway from the Dauntsey Station, on the Main Line of the Great Western Railway, to Malmesbury, with its Terminus four miles from the Town of Tetbury, and with an intermediate station at Great Somerford. The line will be 6¼ miles in length. It will be easy of construction, traversing a level country nearly the entire way; its gradients will, therefore, be good; and it has been laid out in such a manner that the all but unanimous support of the landowners through whose estates it will pass has been obtained.

A careful estimate has been made, which has been verified by the principal Engineer of the Great Western Railway Company, and it is believed that the Capital proposed to be raised will be sufficient to cover all preliminary expenses, and the cost of constructing the Line. Estimates have also been made of the traffic returns which may be expected, and they are such as promise to insure a remunerative dividend to the Shareholders.

The Provisional Committee have, moreover, the gratification of announcing that they have been able to enter into arrangement with the Great Western Company of the most favourable character. The Directors of that Company have agreed to recommend to their Shareholders to subscribe for half the entire Share Capital of the Malmesbury Company, and to work the Line when constructed, at 50 per cent. of the gross receipts; and although this arrangement practically amounts to a guarantee, and the least sanguine estimate of the probable traffic shows that it will produce a far higher return upon the capital, yet, for the further security of the Shareholders, and as a basis for arrangement with certain landowners, the Provisional Committee have thought it desirable to obtain from the Great Western Company such a rebate on the traffic carried by them to and from the Malmesbury Line as will alone secure, when the whole of the Share Capital is subscribed, a *minimum* dividend of 2½ per cent.

It is obvious that a line worked by the Great Western Company in connection with their own main system must give greater facilities to the town and neighbourhood of Malmesbury than can be otherwise secured, and will at the same time afford valuable accommodation to the adjacent town of Tetbury, whilst the arrangements above mentioned, and particularly the large interest of the Great Western Company in the undertaking, are in themselves a guarantee that the line will be efficiently worked, and its capabilities fully developed.

The Provisional Committee, therefore, in recommending this undertaking to the notice of the public, call attention to these its special advantages:—It has the support of the landowners, several of whom have expressed their willingness to accept the price of their land in shares. It is a line which can be economically constructed. Half the Capital only will have to be subscribed by the public. The line will be worked on favourable terms, and so as to afford every accommodation to the district. And, lastly, the shareholders are certain of a *minimum* Dividend of 2½ per cent., although the prospects of the undertaking fully warrant their anticipating a much more remunerative return for their investment.

The want of Railway communication has long had a depressing effect upon the prosperity of Malmesbury and its neighbourhood. From various circumstances, previous efforts to supply this want have failed, but the time and opportunity appear to have now arrived, and the Committee accordingly urge upon the public the advisability of at once embracing the exceptional advantages they have secured.

Applications for Shares in the subjoined Form, will be received by the Solicitors or the Secretary.

To the Provisional Committee of the
Malmesbury Railway.

Gentlemen,

Having paid the sum of into the Wilts and Dorset Bank at Malmesbury to your credit, I hereby apply for and agree to take Shares of £10 each in this undertaking, and I agree to execute the Subscribers' Agreement when requested so to do.

Name ____________

Address ____________

Occupation ____________

Date ____________

SOMERFORD

SCALE 40 FEET TO AN INCH

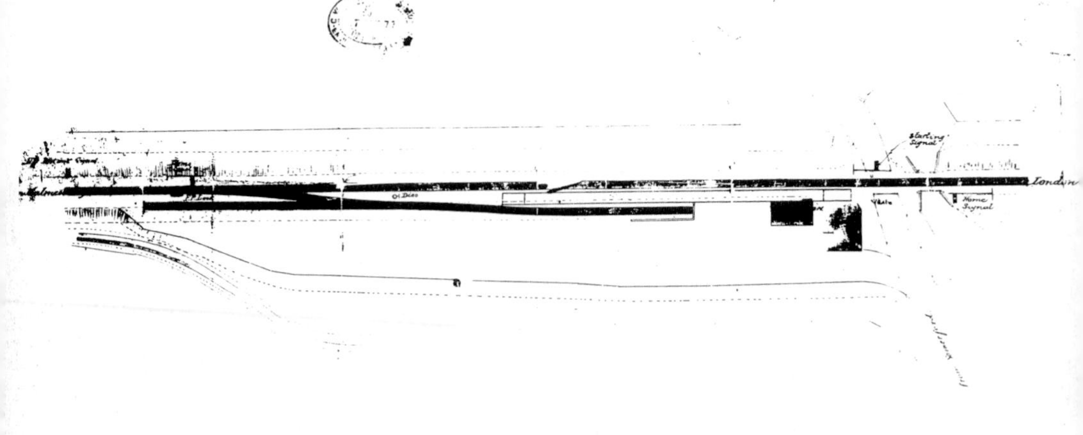

AN EARLY TRACK PLAN of Somerford station (after 1903, Great Somerford) on the Malmesbury branch, its basic facilities about to be increased with the addition of a siding.

lmesbury Railway Station.

THE LITTLE MALMESBURY BRANCH FROM DAUNTSEY could not profess to be anything other than a quiet, dead-end branch built purely for the benefit of the town itself. It terminated some little way short of the actual shopping centre with the remains of the famous abbey visible on the hillside above the railway. In this view the components of the station are shown to advantage, with station buildings, goods shed and engine shed all visible and with the yard including a cordon or gas tank wagon for recharging the reservoirs on passenger stock at a time when gas lighting was standard. (Lens of Sutton.)

RAILWAY STAFF AND OTHER INTERESTED INDIVIDUALS on the platform at the terminus. With the leisurely schedules allowed for the branch trains in the timetable, there would be little hurry to resume work after the camera had been removed. (Lens of Sutton.)

BY THE LATE 1930s the modern 58xx and 48xx series of 0–4–2Ts had taken over most of the branch services. No. 5802 is seen at the terminus in the process of running around its two-coach train. (Lens of Sutton.)

LOCOMOTIVE CREW AND SHUNTER during a brief lull in shunting at Malmesbury. (Lens of Sutton.)

NO. 5800 AT THE TERMINUS on 10.7.1950 with just 14 months left before closure to passenger services. (Lens of Sutton.)

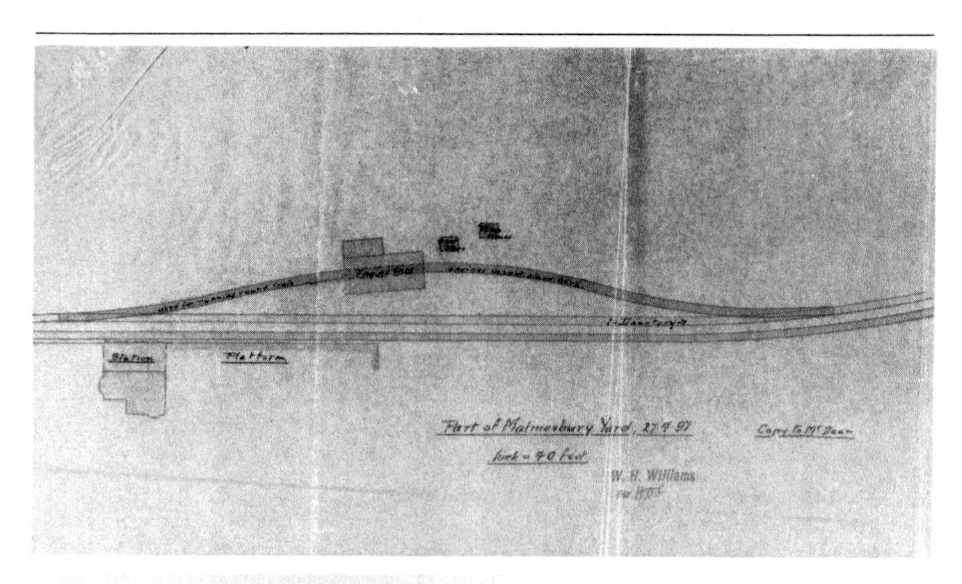

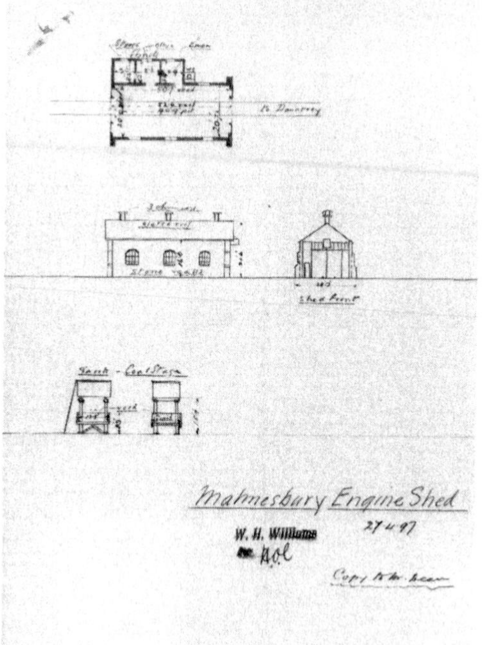

AS WITH TROWBRIDGE records have fortunately survived giving details of the locomotive facilities at the terminus. The information is dated 1897 but is likely to have altered little in the ensuing years.

AS ORIGINALLY BUILT the Malmesbury branch ran almost due north from its junction with the main line at Dauntsey. From 1903 it also passed under the new South Wales direct line just west of Little Somerford station. An alteration to the facilities was made from 1933 when a new connection was provided at Little Somerford into the branch and consequently the original route south was abandoned as a through route. This view shows a portion of the line that was converted to siding status after the construction of a new connection although here it is in good repair complete with fresh ballast. (LGRP)

GREAT WESTERN RAILWA

Particulars of Shed and other accommodation f

ENGINE SHED (*Sketch Plan to be attached*).

How built (Stone, Brick or Wood)	Stone, wood ends slate roof
Inside dimensions. Length	50 7
Breadth	20 7 to 20 0
Height to top of roof ridge ...	21 6
Do. do. wall plate ...	16 0
Cubical contents ...	
Style of Roof (Gable, Hip Gable or Saw-tooth)	Gable
Roof principals (Material)	Wood
If fitted with Smoke Troughs ...	One, full length
Date built, or date Shed was first used ...	
Length of each Line used for running Engines	One 52 0
Do. do. do. repairs ...	None
Engine Pits—Length of each used for running Engines	One 40 6
Do. do. do. repairs ...	None

SHOPS OR OFFICES OUTSIDE THE SHED.

	Stores	Office	Gen. ...
How built (Stone, Brick or Wood) ...	Brick, slate roof	Brick, slate roof	Brick
Inside dimensions. Length	9 0	8 3	
Breadth	8 3	8 2	
Height to top of roof ridge	12 5	12 5	
Do. do. wall plate	9 11	10 0 ceiling	
Cubical contents			
Style of Roof (Gable, Hip Gable or Saw-tooth)	Lean to	Lean to	L
Roof principals (Material)	Wood	Wood	
Date built, or date opened			
Length of Line used for repairs ...			
Do. Engine Pit used for repairs ...			

)MOTIVE DEPARTMENT.

Engines at Malmesbury *Station.*

SIDE SHED.

nes available for standing Engines — None

ngine Pits—length of each … }
Do. at Station … } None

INE TURNTABLES.

iameter … …
ength of Rail … …
irders (Material) …
low turned … …
There fixed … …
ate fixed … …
Maker … …
— None

L. STAGE.

Sketch and size … … 12' 5" x 10' 3" platform

Number of Cranes or Tips … None

How built (Stone, Brick or Wood) Wood on C.I. columns

Date built … …

D FURNACE.

Outside dimensions length. breadth. height

Brief description and Sketch }
Date built … } None
Where situated }

Date Certified 7.2.99 — W. H. Williams Per H.C. Superintendent's Signature.
" " 3.04 — H. Simpson per E.G.W. " "
" " " "
" " " "
" " Copy to Mr. Dean " "

THE MALMESBURY BRANCH TRAIN AT DAUNTSEY *c.* 1921 with a '517' tank in charge of three 4-wheeled coaches. Halcyon days indeed. (Photomatic.)

ANOTHER LITTLE-KNOWN BRANCH IN WILTSHIRE was that from Swindon to Highworth with intermediate stations at Stratton, Stanton and, as depicted here, at Hannington. (HMRS)

LOOKING MORE LIKE A COUNTRY BARN than a railway station the terminus at Faringdon belies the fact that this was once intended to be on a through route to Fairford and Cirencester. Unfortunately railway politics dictated that the various extensions would not be built. The photograph also provides an interesting reminder of how goods were once transported to and from the railway stations, the horse standing patiently whilst the carter and porter pause in their work. (Lens of Sutton.)

LOOKING NOW FROM THE TERMINUS back towards the main line at Uffington and with a decidedly empty-looking yard. The little branch here had a life of 87 years for passenger traffic and like the Malmesbury branch closed in 1951, although goods lingered on for some years to come. (Lens of Sutton.)

Midland & South Western Junction Railway.

Department.

PROBABLY THE MOST COLOURFUL of the independent railway companies in Wiltshire was the Midland and South Western Junction system, itself an amalgamation of two smaller lines. Its main line ran from Cheltenham to Andover, in the course of which it passed through Swindon, much to the chagrin of the GWR which regarded the little company with anything other than favour. Despite this it was amalgamated with the GWR in 1923 although it retained an independent outlook for many years.

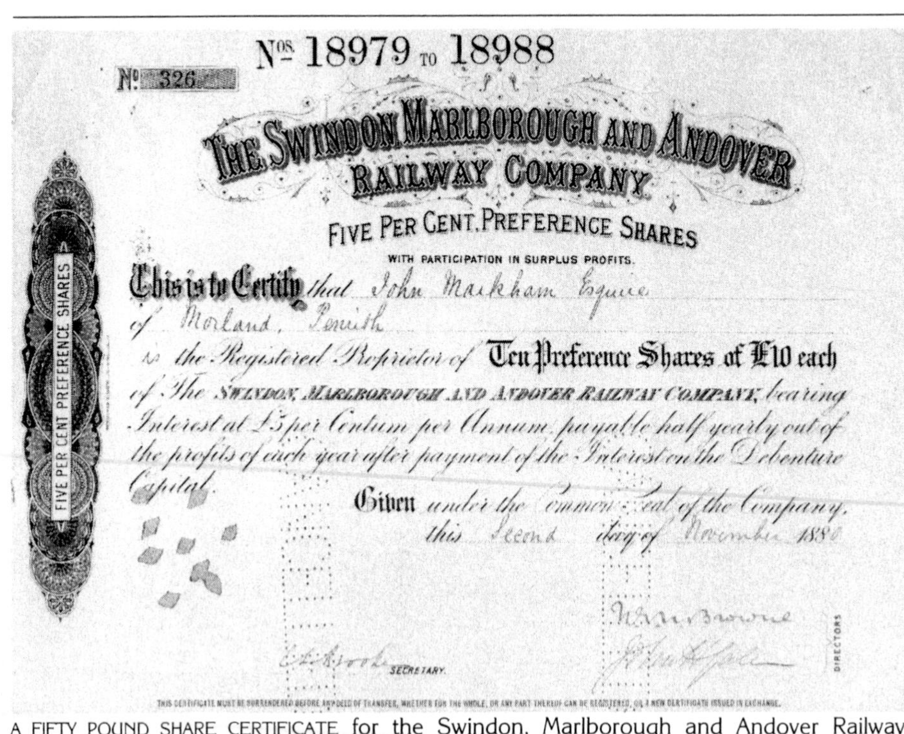
Nos. 18979 to 18988

No. 326

THE SWINDON MARLBOROUGH AND ANDOVER RAILWAY COMPANY

FIVE PER CENT. PREFERENCE SHARES

WITH PARTICIPATION IN SURPLUS PROFITS.

FIVE PER CENT PREFERENCE SHARES

This is to Certify that John Markham Esquire of Morland, Penrith is the Registered Proprietor of Ten Preference Shares of £10 each of The SWINDON, MARLBOROUGH AND ANDOVER RAILWAY COMPANY, bearing Interest at £5 per Centum per Annum, payable half yearly out of the profits of each year after payment of the Interest on the Debenture Capital.

Given under the Common Seal of the Company, this Second day of November 1880

C. L. Brooke SECRETARY.

W. M. Browne
John H. Gale
DIRECTORS

THIS CERTIFICATE MUST BE SURRENDERED BEFORE ANY DEED OF TRANSFER, WHETHER FOR THE WHOLE, OR ANY PART THEREOF CAN BE REGISTERED, OR A NEW CERTIFICATE ISSUED IN EXCHANGE.

A FIFTY POUND SHARE CERTIFICATE for the Swindon, Marlborough and Andover Railway Company of 1880 which, together with the Swindon and Cheltenham Extension Company, was a constituent member of the later MSWJ.

SWINDON, MARLBOROUGH, AND ANDOVER
RAILWAY.

ALLOTMENT LETTER.

Allotment No. 52[a]

Name Laura C Copleston

Address Highfield House, Exmouth

Swindon, 12th January 1875

Madam,

In reply to your application I have the pleasure to inform you that the Directors have allotted to you Two shares in this Company.

Due notice will be given when the Scrip Certificates will be ready for delivery in exchange for this Allotment Letter and Banker's Receipt.

I am, Madam,
Your obedient Servant,

Charles L. Brooke
Secretary.

No certificate has been issued in this case
LB

CANC

A WORLD WAR ONE SCENE at Ludgershall at the southern end of the MSWJ system. Like the other north–south connecting lines to the south coast, the MSWJ carried large quantities of traffic during this period, especially around this end of the line where connections were made to the various army camps fringing Salisbury Plain. (Author's Collection.)

KING GEORGE V inspecting troops at Ludgershall on 8.11.1917. To cater for the royal visit the former Tidworth bay was utilised to stable the royal train, the branch shuttle temporarily departing from the main line platforms. (Lens of Sutton.)

BEING PRIMARILY INTENDED TO DEAL WITH MILITARY TRAFFIC, the platforms at Ludgershall were particularly wide – as witness this view of the facilities in 1906 with part of the Royal Warwickshire Regiment on parade. (Lens of Sutton.)

ANOTHER VIEW showing to advantage the wide expanse of platform at the station as a train from the north passes under the Tidworth road bridge prior to entering the station. Ludgershall was one of the places where locomotives and stock from a variety of different companies could be seen, due to the running of special trains from a number of far-flown destinations. (Lens of Sutton.)

AUSTRALIAN SOLDIERS detrained at Ludgershall in 1916. (Lens of Sutton.)

CONCLUDING THE SEQUENCE ON LUDGERSHALL with a train of early LNWR stock in the platform. Today the railway is still open as far as this point from Andover and carries military traffic on an 'as required' basis. (Lens of Sutton.)

9 67

MIDLAND & SOUTH WESTERN JUNCTION RAILWAY

Number of Station Truck Label ______

Station Truck List.

Between Ludgershall Station Weyhill Station, etc.

2/55 Train, May 19 1923

An Account of Miscellaneous Goods Loaded in the Station Truck, to be conveyed by this Train to the Stations and for the Parties undermentioned, viz.:—

Station Truck Lists are to be dealt with at intermediate Stations in every respect in the same manner as Through Invoices.

Signature ______ *Outwards Clerk.*

Waterlow & Sons Limited, Printers, Dunstable and London.

No. of Truck.	From what Station Invoiced.	To what Station Invoiced.	Name and Address.	Description of Goods.	Mark or No.	The loading Stations to show here at what Station the Guards are to leave the Goods.	Signature of Receiver.
W	Haycroft	Weyhill	Hartigan	House Chairs		Weyhill	[illegible]

MIDLAND & SOUTH WESTERN JUNC. RLY. 22 MAY 1923 SWINDON GENERAL MANAGER'S OFFICE

Signature of Guards working the Station Trucks.		Home of Guard.
	Train from ______ to ______	
	Train from ______ to ______	
	Train from ______ to ______	
	Train from ______ to ______	
	Train from ______ to ______	

Inwards Station ______ Signature ______ Clerk.

INSTRUCTIONS TO BE OBSERVED—AT OUTWARDS STATIONS.

1. A separate list of the goods loaded in each Station Truck must be prepared on Form at the Station where the truck is appointed to start, and the Station Truck List and Invoice must bear the progressive number of the Station Truck Label as shewn in the left-hand margin of the book of Instructions.

2. Goods loaded in the Station Truck during the journey must be entered on the same list when practicable: when not practicable a separate list must be prepared bearing the same progressive number, and be handed to the Guard, who must attach it to the original list.

INSTRUCTIONS TO BE OBSERVED—AT INWARDS STATIONS.

The Agent at the Station to which the Truck is labelled will be responsible for seeing that the Station Truck Lists, when completed, are sent daily to the Stations from which the Trucks commence their journeys with a List of what are sent, which will be returned to the Station certified.

The Lists must be signed at the Outwards and Inwards Stations and by the Guards in the spaces provided for the purpose.

INSTRUCTIONS TO BE OBSERVED—BY GOODS GUARDS.

1. Lists of all Goods loaded in the Station Trucks must be entered by the Stations on the proper Station Truck List Forms, and the Guards must in all cases see that they receive these Lists together with the Invoices of the Goods, and that the Goods correspond with the Lists.

2. To see that all Goods missing, damaged or delayed, are duly noted on the Station Truck Lists; that the signatures are obtained of the men at the various Stations into whose care the Goods are delivered; and the Guards must not under any circumstances affix the names of such persons, as the signatures must be those of the Inspectors, Foremen, or Porters themselves.

3. To enter in their books the progressive numbers of the Station Truck Lists and the Invoices handed over to the person in charge where the Station Trucks are put off, and to obtain his signature for them.

To report on their journals any difficulty in obtaining Station Truck Lists, or signatures for the Goods or Lists, and must make a remark at the back of their journals, and also on the Station Truck Lists, of any case where they find a truck is habitually running with a light load, or which in their opinion can be dispensed with.

JOHN DAVIES, *General Manager.*

A PARTICULARLY INTERESTING PHOTOGRAPH supposedly taken during the construction of the Tidworth branch. The view shows a number of persons descending from the open wagons by means of purpose-built ladders and so could very well be an inspection train on the then as yet incomplete railway. (Lens of Sutton.)

SITUATED AT THE END OF A SHORT BRANCH FROM LUDGERSHALL, the station at Tidworth boasted the highest-ranking station master at any of the MSWJ locations, calculated on the value of military traffic handled. (Valentine Series.)

A LOCAL SERVICE ENTERING TIDWORTH on the shuttle from Ludgershall. Conventional passenger traffic on the line was small and would hardly warrant the number of passenger vehicles shown. (Lens of Sutton.)

AS WITH THE B & H, so the MSWJ stations possessed a style of architecture all of their own; a single storey building with canopy the full width of the platform. Originally much taller chimneys were provided but most were later cut down as shown here. Grafton station was for a brief time the northern terminus of the southern half of the SM & A system; that is until running powers between Marlborough and Grafton were agreed with the independent Marlborough Railway and the GWR. In true railway tradition the station was also some distance away from the village it served. (Author's Collection.)

DUE TO RAILWAY POLITICS two stations emerged at Savernake. This is the high-level site which was in existence as a passenger station for less than 50 years from 1898. Today it is a private residence although the present owner has retained a degree of railway flavour with several items brought in to re-create the atmosphere of years gone by. (LGRP)

NORTH OF SAVERNAKE difficulties with the GWR eventually led the MSWJ to promote and build its own line independently to Marlborough. Unfortunately the geographical terrain was expensive to breach and included the necessity of a tunnel under Savernake Forest. Double track was originally provided although it was later converted to two parallel single lines with one going to Savernake Low Level and the other to the High Level station. (BR)

THE TOWN OF MARLBOROUGH originally boasted two railway stations, one at the terminus of the independent branch from Savernake and the other as shown here on the MSWJ system. This was also one of the few stations other than on a main line to boast a licensed refreshment room, which outlived the railway by a number of years. (Lens of Sutton.)

A VIEW OF MARLBOROUGH MSWJ during a relatively quiet period looking towards Swindon. A legacy of the early days of inter-company rivalry and inadequate funding had meant the line was built on this particular course through the town instead of on a high viaduct to an end-on connection with the existing station. The A345 Marlborough road through Savernake Forest runs under the railway at right angles at the end of the platform. (Author's Collection.)

WHAT PROBABLY MADE THE MSWJ MOST ATTRACTIVE TO THE ENTHUSIAST was that it also possessed its own locomotives and rolling stock, each painted in the company's livery of deep crimson. Later, under the auspices of Swindon, a number of former MSWJ designs were 'westernised', this particular example being a former Beyer Peacock-built 0–6–0 of 1899, seen here with a GWR standard No. 10 boiler and GWR tender. (LGRP)

GWR INFLUENCE in the form of a 'Duke' class 4–4–0 at the head of a southbound goods *c.* 1930. North of Swindon much of the MSWJ system was single track although passing loops were provided at most of the intermediate stations. (Lens of Sutton.)

Midland and South Western Junction Railway.

(170) [W. & S. Ltd.]

TO

CHISELDON

MSWJ HORSEBOXES AT CHISELDON in the early years of this century, the whole scene blending in well with the rural background. Notice the photographer has utilised the end of one of the vehicles to advertise his business. (Lens of Sutton.)

VIEWED TOWARDS MARLBOROUGH with the proximity of the station to the village apparent. (Lens of Sutton.)

ANOTHER OF THE STANDARD DESIGN STATION BUILDINGS was provided at Chisledon although on the opposite platform there was only the basic shelter. The company was keen to exploit the maximum revenue by utilising as much space as possible for advertising. (Lens of Sutton.)

DEEP IN THE HEART OF THE OPPOSITION'S TERRITORY at Swindon and in what is now referred to as the Old Town. Here the MSWJ had its company offices whilst a locomotive shed was also provided south of the station on the way to Chiseldon. (Lens of Sutton.)

A FINAL VIEW OF THE MSWJ with a Sharp, Stewart & Co. 4–4–0T, believed to be just north of Swindon.

SWINDON, MARLBORO' AND ANDOVER RAILWAY.

No. 661 TRAIN STAFF TICKET.

(UP)

Train No. [illegible]

To the Engine Driver [illegible]

You are authorised after seeing the Train Staff for the Section, to proceed from [illegible] to [illegible], and the Train Staff will follow.

Signature of Person in charge [illegible]

Date [illegible] [OVER]

OPENING OF LINES IN DATE ORDER.

31. 5.1841	Swindon, Kemble, Cirencester.
30. 6.1841	London to Bristol throughout. (Individual sections were opened earlier.)
5. 9.1848	Thingley (Chippenham) to Westbury.
7.10.1850	Westbury to Frome.
9.10.1851	Westbury to Warminster.
30. 6.1856	Warminster to Salisbury.
2. 2.1857	Bathampton to Bradford on Avon.
1. 5.1857	Andover to Salisbury.
1. 7.1857	Holt Junction to Devizes.
24. 5.1859	Salisbury Market House Railway.
1. 6.1860	Salisbury to Yeovil.
4.11.1862	Hungerford to Devizes.
29.10.1863	Chippenham to Calne.
14. 4.1864	Savernake to Marlborough.
1. 6.1864	Uffington to Faringdon.
18.12.1877	Dauntsey to Malmesbury.
5. 2.1883	MSWJ system.
9. 5.1883	Swindon to Highworth.
26. 6.1898	Marlborough to Grafton MSWJ.
29. 7.1900	Patney and Chirton to Westbury.
1. 6.1902	Amesbury & Military Camp Light Railway.
1. 7.1902	Ludgershall to Tidworth.
1. 1.1903	Wootton Bassett to Badminton.
1. 6.1906	Amesbury to Bulford.
c. 1917	Military Railway Codford to Sutton Veney.